SHORELINE

More Shelive
for Simone

SHORELINE

three plays by
Don Hannah

Rubber Dolly
Running Far Back
Fathers and Sons

Don Hannah

SIMON & PIERRE
A MEMBER OF THE DUNDURN GROUP
TORONTO · OXFORD

Editor: Marc Côté
Design: Scott Reid
Printer: Webcom

Canadian Cataloguing in Publication Data

Hannah, Don, 1951–
Shoreline: three plays

ISBN 0-88924-290-9
I. Title.

PS8565.A583S56 1999   C812'.54   C99-931950-7
PR9199.3.H36S56 1999

1   2   3   4   5   03   02   01   00   99

THE CANADA COUNCIL | LE CONSEIL DES ARTS
FOR THE ARTS | DU CANADA
SINCE 1957 | DEPUIS 1957

We acknowledge the support of the **Canada Council for the Arts** for our publishing program. We also acknowledge the support of the **Ontario Arts Council** and the **Book Publishing Industry Development Program** of the **Department of Canadian Heritage.**

Printed and bound in Canada.

Printed on recycled paper.

Simon & Pierre
8 Market Street
Suite 200
Toronto, Ontario, Canada
M5E 1M6

Simon & Pierre
73 Lime Walk
Headington, Oxford,
England
OX3 7AD

Simon & Pierre
2250 Military Road
Tonawanda NY
U.S.A. 14150

Shoreline: an introduction by Urjo Kareda

New Brunswick is not simply the place where Don Hannah was born; in a more profound sense, it is where he comes from, and where he creates from. I don't know of anything that he has written in which those roots do not manifest themselves. The three plays gathered in this volume are the testimony to that Maritime centrality. *Rubber Dolly* (premiered in 1986) presents a harrowing portrait of a young woman who has wrenched herself wilfully from her New Brunswick childhood, never to find herself again. *Running Far Back* (1994) — the title is a translation from the Mi'kmaq of Shediac, where Hannah is from — spans almost three decades, and three generations, of a New Brunswick family's struggle toward acceptance and cohesion. *Fathers and Sons* (1998) examines how a boy matures and a man ages, irretrievably out of synch, against the backdrop of the place (New Brunswick again: where else?) that holds them in and draws them back.

Don Hannah, transplanted to Toronto years ago, can't live in the Maritimes and yet can't stop going back either. That ambivalence and contradiction mirror the way that the New Brunswick setting provides a tension for his characters, who act out their own cycles of attraction to and repulsion for the place which bred them. That place is sometimes perceived as an idyll — fairy-tale woods and forests complete with unmenacing bears, or beaches and sandbars that provide lyrical family gatherings. Finding the perfect sand-dollar is an action in two of these plays. The beauty of the Maritime natural world adds enchantment to the simplest physical experiences. Time becomes suspended in this beauty.

The human nature nourished in this setting is of course not particular to the region, but universal in its individual wars between hope and despair, generosity and cruelty, understanding and incomprehension. But Hannah shows us how the realities of Maritime social and economic life, how Maritime history and tradition, can shape and at times warp these lives. These plays show us the legacies of extreme economic hardship and poverty, and long-embraced prejudices. It is a world in flux, constantly re-invented through successive waves of new immigration: note the boat-people who have turned up in *Running Far Back* or the almost mythical black doctor in *Fathers and Sons*. The characters, in their innermost dreams, hope for redemption, but seek at the very least recognition and understanding. As Mildred states it in *Running Far Back*: "I want someone to tell me they're sorry. That's all." The inheritance of discontent and helplessness that builds toward generations, sometimes brings forth brutality and violence: *Rubber Dolly* builds toward the murder of a child, and the killing of a young man launches the action of *Running Far Back*.

The countermovement to these dark downward-spiralling narratives comes from the resilience which Don Hannah cherishes in the Maritime personality. This reveals itself most immediately in the richness of language and verbal traditions of New Brunswick. Through his orchestration of dialect, idiom, vocabulary, rhythm, slang, and adage, Hannah brings the language of the Maritimes unforgettably, in all its variety, onto the Canadian stage. This pungent and energetic language also provides the natural instrument for the uproarious though often bitterly bleak humor which underscores Hannah's work, breaking into wild laughter often at the very darkest moments. Bleak experience and black humor seem co-dependent here.

The other source of regeneration creates the recurrent theme in these works: the complexity of the family relationship, those bonds which can tighten and choke but which also support and nurture. All three plays explore the challenges that a family hurls at its own unity. What is interesting to observe is the difference in style and attack within these linked plays written over a decade-and-a-half.

The earliest, *Rubber Dolly*, is a hard-edged, blunt, elliptical succession of scenes, assembled confrontationally to bring us against — and into — Fern's sense of dislocation and confusion.

Her desperation as an illiterate, unemployed, sometimes abused, single welfare mother is made tactile for us, and yet the writer never reduces her to a statistic. We are brought back time and again to her childhood innocence, a world of games and fantasy, a gentler time when a little girl, returning from a family outing, laughs in her sleep, without waking up, under "the biggest moon I ever seen in my whole life." Her sister Marie also embodies Fern's connection to her roots. Marie is only marginally better off than Fern, but Hannah is keen to define that margin, the tough determination to survive which differentiates the sisters. Marie's love for Fern, despairing but unconditional, is what was seeded in New Brunswick. It is telling, therefore, that when Fern resolves to shape her feelings to positive ends, her imagery is from home, too: "I's crossin that Trans-Canada ta hike back here an I feels alla my love comin back inta me like high tide."

Running Far Back has a more fluid, shimmering structure, advancing often through striking and subtle imagistic gestures and groupings. Don Hannah's cool-eyed examination of the tensions between New Brunswick's anglophone and francophone communities is charged with bruising ironies and missed connections. The older generation fears change, and the young fear that nothing will change. Loretta tries to deny her nature because of the guilt she feels about Louis' murder; she buries that self, symbolized by the watch that her brother Bobby gave her, in sand which will be washed away by the sea. She acts out her defiance by pursuing the "other" — Benoit, the French boy whom she marries and torments — before she grasps that the truly forbidden "other" is her own brother. The play is a love-story in which feelings lie almost fully submerged, surfacing only in dream-like tableaux and an uncovered shard of acceptance at the end. As in *Rubber Dolly*, a small child is held hostage to conflicted adults.

The child and the adult achieve almost archetypal stature in *Fathers and Sons*, the most recent of these plays and the one written in the same time period when Don Hannah was completeing his first major work of fiction, his novel *The Wise and Foolish Virgins*. The writing is both more literary as well as more inward; instead of the intense confrontations of *Rubber Dolly* or the subconscious visions of *Running Far Back*, Hannah provides, in *Fathers and Sons*, a piece of stage-music in four movements, a succession of reflective monologues performed by two actors of the same age, one portraying the journey from babbling infancy to maturity, the other the journey from youthful parenthood to senility and death. This latest variation on the New Brunswick worldscape feels gentler, more like a fable. If a Don Messer tune was the ideal musical correlative in *Rubber Dolly*, and "Lipstick on your collar" the apt adolescent anthem of *Running Far Back*, then it seems appropriate that *Fathers and Sons* should incorporate the sophisticated elegance of Biber's *Mystery Sonata* for solo violin (played live by one of the play's characters). Historic and socio-cultural events now assume a tall-tale quality, whether it's the coming of the circus, or the arrival of margarine in the Maritimes, or the secrets of the Freemasons. Even the union of Allen and Helena — perhaps the only happy marriage in Hannah's work — seems charmed, a chivalric romance. In this world of reverie, despite the inevitable missed connections, the final feeling is one of generous reconciliation.

If that reconciliation is a new element in Don Hannah's plays, the compassion that generates it is not. It has always been there. Fern in *Rubber Dolly* may commit the unspeakable, but she remains embraced by the playwright's tenderness. It is because he so fully understands the world that she comes from — which is where he, too, comes from — that he can place her on that beautiful and yet brutal shore, and also elevate her above it, as if lifted upward by a tidal wave.

For Ken Garnhum

Listen! you hear the grating roar
Of pebbles which the waves draw back, and fling,
At their return, up the high strand,
Begin, and cease, and then again begin,
With tremulous cadence slow, and bring
The eternal note of sadness in.

MATTHEW ARNOLD
"Dover Beach"

Rubber Dolly

for Pat, Laura, Ruby, Ray, Duke and Sappo

Cast

FERN, age 15–23
MARIE, her sister, nine years older
JOEY, age 6, Fern's son
JOE, 18 to 23
FRED, 25
A SAILOR
ANNA, in her thirties

Joe, Fred, and the Sailor *must* be played by the same actor.

The present day ("Now") of the play is the mid 1980s.

Set

Lighting is crucial for "Rubber Dolly." The set should be as simple as possible. At the back, a wall with two doors. In one area, a table and chairs for tavern and kitchen scenes. A raised area for Joey.

"Rubber Dolly" was first presented by Tarragon Theatre, Toronto on November 21, 1986, with the following cast:

Fern	Kim Renders
Marie	Michelle Fisk
Joey	Thomas Barber
Joe, Fred, Sailor	Peter Krantz
Anna	Lynne Deragon

Set and Lights	Jim Plaxton
Costumes	Melanie Huston
Stage Manager	Anne Thompson

The play was directed by JoAnna McIntyre

"Rubber Dolly" received workshop preparation and presentation at the Tarragon Theatre, the Theatre Resource Centre, and the Banff Playwrights Colony.

SCENE ONE

[FERN, *now. The Institution. A cold light. Lights soften during her speech and become dappled, a forest.*]

FERN   When I runs away that time when I was fifteen? I lived in the ravine back a Riverdale Farm. I slept in a tree.

Very first time I runs away I's just a little kid and I hid in a woods. It felt real nice there. It's where I used a play with Donna and Marie 'fore they growed up and left me. We used a play this dumb thing called "Barbie's Vacation" where we took the dolls into the woods and made like they was campin' in tents made out a Dad's handkerchiefs and the dishtowels. They changed their clothes a lot and we pushed their feets into the ground so they stood up. They was pretty. Like pictures in a catalogue? Like that. Aunt Marsha always made Barbie clothes for Christmas and stuff, but once on my birthday I gots this real pant suit with sequins and a little hat. It was a dumb thing for Barbie to wear on vacation, but like I says to Donna and Marie, it was okay if she's just campin' on her ways to somewheres else. Like maybe China? Marie said China's far away as ya could get, so far 'way it was straight down. Sammy was always out by the lilacs diggin' holes to China.

Anyways, that's where I's hiding, and for a long time too, cause I figured they'd be lookin' everywheres for me. This kid from Down Shore run way once and they had search parties like they had for the prisoners from Dorchester. I figured all a my brothers and sisters'd be lookin' for me. I got twelve brothers and sisters and I was the littlest, 'cept for Sammy. I donno how many grandchildren there is no more — we was all gonna get together once but my brothers always beat up on each other when they's drinkin' and nobody talks to Donna.

So I was hidin' there in a woods, and I ate all a my chips and talked to Barbie and it was real nice till it was gettin' dark and I hears a noise like sticks breakin', and I thought, "Jeezo, that's the bear!" Just like Grampy always said there'd be: this big brown bear comes walkin' out a the woods. I didn't dare breathe and he walks right past me. I's so ascared I counts t'a hundred and I takes off. When I told Mom she didn't believe me, just gimme the wooden spoon for gettin' my pants wet. Nobody even knowed I run aways till I told Donna it's a secret, and she told Mom, and Mom beat me again and stuck me in the dark closet all day. Said it'd serve a little liar like me right if there was a bear and he bites my stupid head off.

So when I runs away that time when I was fifteen, I come to Toronto and slept in the ravine. Mom thoughts I was at my sister's, my big sister Marie's, and I told Marie I was livin' with Jean, but really I was down in the ravine. Jean was my best friend back then. I met'r on the train comin' up here. When I told her I gots twelve brothers and sisters, she laugh some hard cause she come from Moncton, didn't have no big family.

I never laugh so much as that summer I come

up here on the train. Me and Jean's best friends right aways. We met these guys who was sailors on the train and we laugh all night long. One of them's called Frank and he was so smart. He showed me a picture of himself they took on some island in Europe. I was a little ascared. Cripes, I was only fifteen. But he didn't know that cause I had on make-up and everything. He put his arm on me real tight and called me "baby," just like guys did just in songs I thought.

It was romantic out there 'tween the cars. We was goin' by Quebec or some place at night. Maybe it sounds cheap, but it weren't cause he was so nice to me, and we was on a train, and there was moonlight and everything. Like in a movie? Only better. We almost got caught by a conductor, but my sailor was holdin' me real tight and whisperin' that he won't let nothin' bad happen to me ever.

I never ever seen'm again, but that sailor was so nice to me.

No guys back in New Brunswick'd ever think to call you "baby."

[*Train whistle faintly in the distance. A* SAILOR *appears in the dim light by the train door.*]

Rubber Dolly

SCENE TWO

[*Music fades in, "Rubber Dolly" by Don Messer. Lights up slowly on* JOEY *(age 6) lying on a raised area. His jacket is bunched up under his head for a pillow. While the chorus plays,* JOEY *sits up, does a vaudeville routine with the jacket. He wears it like Superman's cape, shakes it like a bullfighter, drapes it over his head and walks like a monster.*]

TAPE   My Mommy told me
if I'd be goodie
that she would buy me
a rubber dolly
so don't go tell her
I've got a feller
or she won't buy me
a rubber dolly.

SCENE THREE

[FERN*'s apartment. A year and a half ago.*]

FERN   Joey, c'mon! I already took your sister 'cross the hall and I promise the teachers ya wouldn't be late no mores.
C'mon.

[JOEY *is playing with a Masters of the Universe He Man doll.*]

JOEY   Yeah, yeah.

FERN   C'mon. Teacher said you's doin' good in school.

JOEY   You know what? Me and Josh built a fort!

17

FERN   Yeah? You know there's no black kids when I was little? I never seen no black people when I was a kid. I never seen a real one till I come to Toronto. Just pictures.

JOEY   How come?

FERN   There weren't none.

JOEY   Where was they?

FERN   They was here, maybe. Or Jamaica. And there's no Chinamans neither where I growed up.

JOEY   Grew up.

FERN   Just white people. There was English and French white people.

JOEY   We gots this new kid at school. He's from this new place called Louse.

FERN   Where's that? I ain't never heard a no place called Louse.

JOEY   There's a big war there. He seen it. And they had to throw pigs off the boats at night cause they was too noisy.

FERN   Yeah? Put on your coat.

JOEY   He's Chinese, sort a, he's funny. Can he come for supper?

FERN   No, not today.

JOEY   Tomorrow?

FERN   I don't know, now put on your coat.

JOEY   Why can't he come for supper?

FERN   Cause I said so. Now, put on your coat. I promise the teacher you'd wear it everyday now.

JOEY   When can he come for supper?

FERN   Joey, don't ask me now, okay?

JOEY   No fair, you're mean.

FERN   Lookit, I'm tired. Just put on your coat, baby.

JOEY   No. I didn't have to wear no coat at the foster home.

FERN   I don't care 'bout what you did at no foster home.

JOEY   They was nice to me there. Better than you.

FERN   Quit it or I'll send you back.

JOEY   Good.

FERN   Just put on your coat, will you?

JOEY   They was nicer than you.

FERN   Put on your coat now!

JOEY   No! Make me!

FERN   Put on the coat!

JOEY   No way José.

FERN	Will you just put on the fuckin' coat!
JOEY	Ohoh, Mommy said the "f" word.
FERN	PUT IT ON NOW!
JOEY	You can't make me.
FERN	Quit it!
JOEY	They said you're bad.
FERN	*(Explodes)* PUT THAT THING ON OR I'LL HIT YA!
JOEY	*(Laughs)* You can't make me, you can't make me!

[FERN *tries to grab him, but he runs away from her.*]

JOEY	You can't catch me, you can't catch me!
FERN	STAND STILL, I'M GONNA GIVE YOU THE WOODEN SPOON!
JOEY	Na nana na naaaaa!

[JOEY *is still laughing when* FERN *grabs him. Blackout.*]

SCENE FOUR

[MARIE*'s kitchen, seven years ago.* FERN *(15) is drinking a bottle of beer.* MARIE *(24) is ironing.*]

MARIE	Can't you use a glass?

[FERN *rolls her eyes and drinks from the bottle.*]

MARIE   It just looks bad, that's all.

FERN   It's how they drink in movies sometimes.

MARIE   Well, this ain't a movie, it's my kitchen. Ya looks cheap.

FERN   F'I use a glass'll I looks expensive?

MARIE   Oh, Jeez, you're hopeless.

FERN   Shit.

MARIE   I mean it. Mom ever finds out I let a kid like you drink —

FERN   I don't wanna hear 'bout Mom, I's sick a her.

MARIE   You got a big chip on your shoulder 'bout Mom.

FERN   She put it there.

MARIE   Mom didn't have it easy.

FERN   Aw, too bad, aw ...

MARIE   She didn't have no easy life.

FERN   Aw, gee, aw ...

MARIE   Quit it.

FERN   Shit Marie, she's a old bitch.

21

MARIE	She didn't have no easy life.
FERN	That's tough, that's real tough. Smartest thing I ever did's get out a that dump. Bunch a assholes. You's smart enough to get out. Dumb assholes.
MARIE	God knows we was poor, but that's no reason to talk like that.
FERN	*(Mimics)* "God knows we was poor." Aw, you sound just like her. "God knows we was poor, but ya always had food on the table." Christ, she couldn't pan-fry shit for a tramp.
MARIE	Hey!
FERN	"God knows we was poor, but that kitchen floor was always dirty as sin."
MARIE	Quit it.
FERN	*(Giggles)* "God knows we was poor, but your father whored around every night of his life!"
MARIE	You never gonna grow up?
FERN	I'm grown up.
MARIE	"I'm grown up." Jeez. That's a hot one.
FERN	I moved out a home, didn't I?
MARIE	Big Deal.
FERN	I did.

MARIE You just moved out last week, let's see how long you last on your own.

FERN I'm old enough to have kids. I can have babies.

MARIE "I can have babies." Jeez, Fernie, monkeys can have babies. You got no more brains than God gave a hen. Don't you dare have kids, don't you dare. Jeezo Cripes.

FERN You weren't much older than me.

MARIE What do you know? And anyways, I was eighteen. Eighteen! You ain't even sixteen yet. "Have babies." Cripes! Don't go lookin' for trouble. Look for work instead.

FERN Aw, here we goes.

MARIE Well, Gerrard Street weren't paved with gold last time I seen it. Whatcha gonna do for money? You and that precious girlfriend of yours.

FERN Jean's gettin' Unemployment.

MARIE Well you ain't 'cause you never worked. You been to see the lady at the Dominion? Aw Cripes, Fernie, and I got Doris to tell her you'd be over.

[FERN *rolls her eyes.*]

MARIE What's the matter? Oh, I suppose you're too good now to work at a grocery store. Well, that's a good job.

FERN So you take it.

MARIE: Oh, sure. And you gonna stay here all day and look after my two kids I bet.

FERN   Me and Jean's gonna work at the Ex.

MARIE   The Ex! Don't be stupid. Two or three weeks work that's all that is. Go see the Dominion lady. That job lasts a lifetime.

FERN   I don't wanna work at no dumb Dominion store for a lifetime.

MARIE   Oh, talkin' to you's like talkin' to the floor.

FERN   That's cause you walk all over me all the time.

MARIE   Oh, poor li'l Fernie. Jeezo. Stop feelin' sorry for yourself, will ya? Get a job. You wanna get treated like a grown up, act like one for a change.

FERN   You hates me almost as much as Mom.

MARIE   Oh, turn the record over.

FERN   She never picked on you.

MARIE   What do you know? You's just a li'l kid. Mom didn't treat me no different. She didn't have time for favourites.

FERN   She didn't have time for nothin'.

MARIE   Just 'cause she didn't sit around all day like a big fool sayin' "I love ya, I love ya" don't mean she didn't. She loved us all the same, every last one of us.

24

FERN   Same as what?

MARIE   Oh, you're hopeless.

FERN   Bet she didn't tell you you's the last friggin' thing on earth she needs. Stupid old bitch should never had no kids.

MARIE   If Mom never had no kids, you wouldn't be sittin' around in Toronto drinkin' your sister's beers.

FERN   I said I'd pay you back when I'm workin'.

MARIE   *(Stacking laundry in basket)* When's that gonna be? The day you's buyin' I'll be too old to drink.

FERN   Me and Jean's gonna work at the Ex.

MARIE   Yeah.

FERN   I'm goin' there tomorrow.

MARIE   Yeah, sure.

FERN   You callin' me a liar?

MARIE   Just go talk to the Dominion lady, will ya? Cripes, try growin' up.

                [MARIE *exits.*]

SCENE FIVE

[*A tavern, seven years ago. Country music on the jukebox.* FERN *(15) sits at a table, puts on lipstick, fixes her hair.* JOE *(18) enters, slightly*

25

drunk, carrying two bottles of beer. He goes to FERN.]

JOE   Hi, Pussycat, anyone sittin' there?

FERN   Just my girlfriend Jean, but she ain't here yet. She's late.

JOE   So you're waitin' all alone there.

FERN   Yeah, I guess.

JOE   You wanna beer?

FERN   Yeah, sure. You wanna sit down?

JOE   Yeah *(Grins, handing* FERN *a beer)* Take a load off my mind, eh? *(Sits)*

FERN   I seen you before.

JOE   Yeah?

FERN   I seen you 'round. Your name's Joe.

JOE   Yeah. You seen me, eh?

FERN   Yeah. 'Round.

JOE   I seen you too. Around. You're pretty girl.

FERN   Yeah?

JOE   Yeah. You got a name, pretty girl?

FERN   Course I got a name. Fern.

26

JOE   Fern. Fern, eh? That's a pretty name, too. Like them green things.

FERN   Yeah. Ferns. I don't understand why my girlfriend Jean's so late. She's always here first.

JOE   Yeah? Maybe she got lucky, eh?

                   [FERN *shrugs.*]

JOE   You wanna glass there?

FERN   Oh, yeah, sure.

                   [JOE *takes a draft glass from his pocket.*]

JOE   I was gonna take this home till I saw you sittin' here all alone.

FERN   Yeah?

                   [FERN *accepts the glass, and pours some beer into it.*]

JOE   Yeah.

                   [*They drink.*]

JOE   So. How come I just started to see you here?

FERN   I just move here.

JOE   Yeah? Where's ya come from, Fern? Hollywood?

FERN   Down east.

JOE   Oh, Newfie, eh?

FERN   No.

JOE   Oh, sorry.

FERN   That's okay. New Brunswick.

JOE   Oh.

FERN   Near Moncton.

JOE   Yeah? Well, you know what I say? You know
            what? I say you're too pretty lookin' for down
            there, eh? That's what I say.

            [FERN *shrugs.*]

JOE   So what you think of that, eh?

            [FERN *smiles, shrugs.*]

JOE   Know what else I say there, eh?

FERN   What?

JOE   You're real quiet.

FERN   Yeah?

JOE   Yeah. 'Bout as quiet as y'are pretty.

FERN   Not what my sister says.

JOE   No?

            [FERN *shakes her head.*]

JOE   This sister ever met you?

FERN	Course she met me. Where you from?
JOE	Me? I ain't from nowheres.
FERN	No?
JOE	No, I always live here. Over on Ontario Street.
FERN	Yeah? I never met no one from Toronto before.
JOE	No?
FERN	No. Just people from somewheres else who lives here.
JOE	Oh. Say, can I bum a smoke there?
FERN	Oh, yeah, sorry.

[*She holds out her pack and he takes three cigarettes.*]

JOE	Why keep askin', eh?
FERN	Yeah, I guess.

[*As if it were the most sophisticated gesture in the world,* JOE *takes the cigarette from her hand and uses it to light his own.*]

JOE	So, Fern, your girlfriend didn't show up yet, eh?
FERN	Yeah. Ya know, I don't understand. Jean's never late, nevers.
JOE	What'd she do if she got here and you was gone?

FERN   Where'd I be?

JOE   Say ya got lucky.

FERN   Yeah?

JOE   Yeah.

FERN   Yeah, how lucky?

JOE   Lucky as you want.

FERN   Jeez.

JOE   What?

FERN   Well, you don't beat around the bush much.
          Jeez.

JOE   No. I'm fast Joey, eh? And you're a pretty girl,
          Fern.

FERN   Yeah? I betcha say that lots.

JOE   Maybe. But say this time I ain't kiddin' around.

FERN   Jeez, I donno. Like I's supposed to meet Jean
          and everythin'.

JOE   *(Touches her)* Meet Jean tomorrow. Tell her
          tomorrow. Call her up. Say ya got lucky.

FERN   Jeez, like I seen you before and everythin' but ...

JOE   Know what I say? I say your friend got lucky.
          She was walkin' over here and she got lucky.
          This here's a lucky day for ya both. And me too.

30

[JOE *leans over to kiss her.*]

JOE   There. How 'bout that? Ya make me feel real happy.

FERN   Yeah? Aw. No shit.

JOE   Hey, would I be shittin' you?

FERN   I donno.

            [*He stares at her. She meets his look, then turns away.*]

JOE   Baby?

FERN   I donno.

JOE   Would I shit ya?

FERN   Naw, I guess. Naw, ya wouldn't.

JOE   That's right.

            [*He kisses her again, deeper.*]

JOE   Eh? C'mon, baby.

            [*They butt their cigarettes in the ashtray. He takes her arm and stands. As the music rises, they stand together, kissing. Fade to black.*]

SCENE SIX

[MARIE's *kitchen. Six months later.*]

MARIE   Handin' out cotton candies for a couple of

weeks last summer ain't workin'. You keep throwin' that round like you had somethin'. You's just a couple of kids makin' goo-goo eyes at some bums buyin' candy.

FERN   What a you know?

MARIE   Lots, I know lots. Lookie here, all y'ever do is hand round with that Jean and —

FERN   Whatcha mean, *that* Jean? Whatcha got against Jean?

MARIE   Sorry, sorry. I should just keep my big mouth shut.

FERN   What's wrong with her?

MARIE   Forget it, forget I ever said a thing.

FERN   No, I won't. You do this all the goddam time. Christ. What's wrong with her?

MARIE   Look, I'm just sick a you gettin' led around by that hotshot Jean. She says "Jump" you says "How high?" All I ever hear is "Jean this" and "Jean that."

FERN   Jean's the best friend I ever had.

MARIE   She talks big.

FERN   So what? She s'posed to *(tiny voice)* "talk little?"

MARIE   Big talkers, both a ya. And that bum Joe ya think's such a hot shit.

FERN	He ain't no bum!
MARIE	Oh, Fernie. He ought a have a sign over'm with big red letters — "I'M A BUM."
FERN	Shut up!
MARIE	No, you grow up. He ain't workin', is he? All he does is hang out at a tavern all day and half the night. He's a bum.
FERN	He's lookin'.
MARIE	Yeah? For what?
FERN	For a job.
MARIE	For a job. Jeez. I'll tell ya what he's lookin' for. He's lookin' for a drink.
FERN	He's lookin' for a job. He's a roofer.
MARIE	A roofer! Jeezo Cripes!
FERN	Ya seen his jacket, one that says, "'Bove all ya need a roof." He's a roofer.
MARIE	Ha! That jacket should say "'Bove all I'm a bum!" Just cause that bum stands round like Popeye from the comic books wigglin' his big arms, you believes anythin' he says.
FERN	So now you're pissed off cause he's in good shape.
MARIE	Don't be so stupid! He cares more about those big arms a his than he cares bout anythin' else. Includin' roofin'. Includin' you!

33

FERN   You're just jealous.

MARIE   Jealous? A that? Don't make me laugh.

FERN   You're jealous cause your husband took off.

MARIE   He didn't take off, I threw him out.

FERN   You're jealous.

MARIE   Nobody can tell you nothin', ya knows it all.

FERN   You're just jealous, you're just jealous —

MARIE   Oh, grow up, will ya? Jeez. I just wanna be round here the day you grows up. But I ain't gonna live to see it —

FERN   *(Chants)* You're just jealous, Marie is jealous!

MARIE   Nobody lives that long.

                [*Blackout.*]

                SCENE SEVEN

                [JOE *and* FERN*'s kitchen, about six months later. Morning.* FERN *is on the telephone.*]

FERN   He did? Aw Jean. *(Laughs)* So what'd ya say? ... *(Giggles)* Yeah?... Naw, I ain't really said nothin' yet. I think maybe he knows though ... I donno, he's actin' funny ... Sure he'll be happy. *(She feels her stomach.)* He'll get used to it. *(Giggles)* Fuck'm if he don't, eh? That's what I say. *(Laughs)*

                [JOE *comes out of the bedroom door, barely awake*

and hung over. He's fastening his jeans.]

FERN   *(Ignores* JOE*)* So ya said what? *(Laughs)* No, fuck him ... Yeah? Well, fuck her. *(Laughs)*

JOE   Fuck.

[JOE *makes fun of the way she's holding the phone.*]

FERN   *(To Jean)* What? Fuck you.

JOE   *(Mimics)* "Fuck you."

FERN   *(Makes a face at* JOE*)* What?... Fuckin' right.

JOE   Oh, fuck.

FERN   *(Makes another face, ignores him)* What?

JOE   I said, "FUCK!"

FERN   What?... No, s'nothin'. Just Joe.

JOE   *(Grabs the receiver from her and throws it.)* Shut the fuck up!

FERN   Hey! Joe, Jesus —

JOE   *(He picks up the phone and hollers into it)* Shut the fuck up! *(Slams down the receiver.)*

FERN   I's just talkin' on the phone for —

JOE   You was talkin' on *my* phone! *(He slaps her face.)* Just fuck off!

FERN   Hey! What's the matter — you gone retarded?

JOE	You fuckin' deaf? I said fuck off.
FERN	What's the —
JOE	Go live with your laugh ass friends.
FERN	You're fuckin' crazy, you're talkin' crazy —
JOE	You're a liar! *(He tries to slap her.)*
FERN	Hey!

[FERN *slaps him and runs to the other side of the table. They chase each other around it.*]

JOE	Fuck! Liar! Fuckin' liar! Ya lie when ya tells me ya's eighteen, too? Jailbait liar!
FERN	*(Sticks out her tongue)* Least I ain't never been to jail.
JOE	You're such a fuckin' baby they wouldn't let you in. Stand still!
FERN	Leave me or I'll call the cops.
JOE	Who'd listen to you? Last night ya weren't callin' the fuckin cops, baby.
FERN	Last night ya wasn't fuckin' retarded.
JOE	Last night I was drunk.
FERN	Oh, big fuckin' surprise! Name me a night when you wasn't!
JOE	Must a been blind fuckin' drunk the night I let

36

you in here. Should a left you livin' in the
fuckin' ravine last summer, ya fuckin' squirrel.

FERN   Fuckin' thief!

JOE   Fuckin' bitch!

FERN   Fuckin' crook!

JOE   Fuckin' retard! Dumbfuck stand still!

FERN   *(Sticks out her tongue)* Run, run, fast as you can,
ya can't catch me, ya fuckin' turd!

JOE   I'm gonna break your fuckin' neck!

        [JOE *trips over a chair and falls.* FERN *runs out
        the door.*]

JOE   OW! FUCK! My fuckin' foot!

FERN   *(Sticks her head back in the door)* Hey, you
fuckin' okay?

JOE   You made me break my fuckin' foot!

FERN   Aw, poor widdle Joy, he bwoke his fuckin' foot.
Aw. Hey! Fuckhead! Walk on *this*!

        [*She gestures with her finger and slams the door.*]

JOE   FUCK YOU! I ain't payin' for no fuckin' kid! Ya
hear me? Shit, fuckin' shit!

        [*Blackout.*]

SCENE EIGHT

[MARIE, *alone.*]

MARIE   Hey, 'member when Donna and me used a
drive ya crazy with them Barbie dolls? We used
a go out back past the fields one summer and
play "Barbie Goes Swimmin'" *(Laughs)* We'd
take the clothes off a the Barbies and you'd get
mad cause we didn't have no bathin' suits for
them. Then we'd throw them in the creek like
they was divers. Jeez, you was funny. You
couldn't reach'm and you's always such a scardy
cat 'bout gettin' wet, so we'd keep tossin' them
in and makin' them swim under waters.
(Giggles) Then Donna'd start talkin' in that
funny little Barbie voice. *(Mimics)* "Lookit me, I
can swim, I can swim." Oh, she was so stupid
soundin' back then before all that crap with that
guy from the liquor store's wife. I can still hear
her. *(Mimics)* "Lookit me, I can swim, I can
swim, oh help me Fernie, I'm drownin', I'm
drownin'!" And she'd throw old Barbie in again
and you'd cry and scream blue murder. *(Laughs)*
Then, then the best part — we'd take them out
a the water and shake them round like this *(She
shakes invisible maracas)* so you'd hear the water
inside of them, and we'd sing that funny song.
(Sings) "La Cucaracha, la cucaracha,
dadadadadadada." 'Member? And when you
heard that water splashin' inside them you'd just
get crazy. So we'd hold'm way up here so ya
couldn't reach.

Aw, maybe we was mean teasin' you like that,
Fernie, but Jeezo, you should a seen how funny
you looked. You was so funny when you got

mad back then. Jeez, you's cute. *(Shakes maracas)* La Cucaracha. Jeez.

[*Blackout.*]

SCENE NINE

[FERN, *now.*]

FERN   When Joey's real little, I used a sing to him some. But he's so smart, he knows I can't sing good, so I quit it when he's about four.

[JOEY *has appeared in his space. He holds a jacket. FERN sees him.*]

FERN   Joey? Hi Joey. It cold there? You gots enough clothes? S'it cold?

[JOEY *drops the jacket.*]

FERN   Aw. Hey, I betcha don't even need your old coat no mores. Hey? Bet that makes ya happy, eh? No more Mommy buggin' ya to put your coat on or nothin'. Is Grampy there? Member when ya fell in at the farm down east and gots all dirty? Ya fell in with them pigs, 'member? You's so little and cute.

JOEY   I was ascared. You got mad at me.

FERN   Aw, I weren't real mad.

JOEY   You was real mad. You hit me. They was big pigs.

FERN   Aw, baby.

JOEY   You're bad.

FERN   Don't say that.

                [JOEY *turns away from her.*]

                Hey, hey, Joey? Oh, jeez. Don't stay mad with
                me, eh? Joey? Don't stay mad.

                'Member that worker we kind a liked? Betty?
                One named Betty? She took us to McDonald's
                once when you's little? 'Fore your sister was
                born, 'fore Jenny? 'Member? And we's all gettin'
                on so well and laughin' so I says somethin' 'bout
                that swimmin' teacher lady at the centre?
                'Member her? I's thinkin' that us and Betty's
                gettin' to be friends and so I says somethin'
                mean 'bout the swimmin' lady, ya know, 'bout
                them legs a hers like a fat cowboy's?

                Aw, please listen to me.

                We was at McDonald's and I says somethin'
                mean and Betty starts treatin' me like a little
                kid. Like she was too good all a sudden. And I
                got real mad. I betcha 'member that part, eh?
                When Mommy got all mad and picked up
                Betty's jumbo pop and fired it at her?

                I was wrong to do it, Joey. I was mad at her
                and I didn't think. Don't be like that, eh?
                Don't stay mad.

                You was the prettiest baby.

JOEY   I hate you.

40

FERN   Aw no. No.

            Ask me somethin'. Ask me one a them stupid
            questions you used to ask. Like "Is Superman
            real?" or "Did I know Elvis?" or stuff like that.
            'Member?

            Aw, you 'members and you's just teasin' me,
            huh?

            [*She looks at him for a moment.*]

            How come you looks different?

JOEY   Guess.

FERN   You looks like your father now, you looks like
            Joe.

JOEY   I was lookin' too much like you. I changed. I
            look like Daddy now.

FERN   Aw, baby, why? You never even knew him.

JOEY   Nobody's gonna know you're my Mommy no
            more.

FERN   Joe never wanted to know you. He left you.

JOEY   No he didn't. He left you.

FERN   You's mean to say that.

JOEY   *(Chants)* I'm a meanie
            Bite my weeny
            I'm a meanie —

FERN   Leave me.

JOEY   Nope.

FERN   Run away like you used to.

JOEY   No way. You come here.

            [*Lights fade on* JOEY.]

FERN   Joey? Baby?

            [*Lights change to next scene.*]

            SCENE TEN

            [*A park, early evening, two years ago.*]

FERN   Joey? Joey?

            [JOE *comes out of the darkness, holding the bag of glue he has been sniffing.*]

FERN   Joey!

JOE   "Joey!"

FERN   Oh! Fuck you scared me!

JOE   You lose somethin' there, baby?

FERN   Why you doin' that shit?

JOE   You lose my fuckin' kid?

FERN   *Your* kid? *My* kid's late for supper's all.

42

JOE	"My kid's late for supper's all." What time you eat supper, eh?
FERN	Joey?
JOE	I asked a fuckin' question.
FERN	I ain't feedin' you if that's what you're gettin' at.
JOE	Ooh, Tough Girl. What time you feed my kid?
	[*She starts to move away and* JOE *grabs her.*]
JOE	Fuckin' answer the fuckin' question!
FERN	Six.
JOE	I can't hear you.
FERN	Six! Fuckin' six six six!
JOE	Six, eh? Well, I say he's real late for supper. Supper's real cold, real fuckin' cold.
FERN	Let go.
JOE	Maybe someone fuckin' took him. Maybe he's locked up in some crazy fridge.
FERN	Joe, fuck off.
JOE	You know what I think? You fuckin' know what I fuckin' think?
FERN	Let me go!
JOE	I think I better help you look for him.

FERN   You leave him alone. You didn't want him five years ago, you leave him alone now. I'll find him.

JOE   *(He lets her go during this)* "I'll find him." You's a fuckin' fuck of a mother, big fuckin' unfit mother. I know why you's only drinkin' in the east end. Eh? You know why?

FERN   So tell me, Mr. Smart Fuck.

JOE   Ain't you comical there, eh? Real funny. You ain't allowed to drink round here cause you're on the fuckin' Indian List.

FERN   You're full a shit.

[*She moves away. He grabs her again.*]

JOE   You know what I say? You know what I fuckin' say? I say I'm gonna call the fuckin' Aid get my kid back. Bet they'd gimme the other one too, eh? A girl, ain't it? Eh? Eh?

FERN   Yeah! Let go!

JOE   You lose them bein' stupid or they just take off on ya? They hates you and just takes off on you, eh?

FERN   Shut up and let go a me!

JOE   You stupid fuck! What good are you? What can you teach them? How to suck cock? That's all you're good for. You gonna turn my son into some kind a cock sucker?

[FERN *starts to struggle. She hits him.*]

44

JOE
You stupid cunt! You got a stupid fuckin' mouth! I hears what you says about me. Big stupid mouth.

[FERN *breaks free and runs off.*]

FERN
Fuck you asshole! Joey! Joey!

JOE
(Goes back to his glue bag) I'm gonna call the fuckin' Children's Aid! Call the Aid on you! Get my fuckin' kid back! Fuck you! Fuckin' bitch, liar, cunt. Fuckin' fuckin' fuckin' fuck ...

[*Blackout.*]

Scene Eleven

[MARIE's. *That night.*]

MARIE
Nobody'd give a kid to that guy — wouldn't give him a dog. You're just talkin' crazy 'cause you're upset.

FERN
Yeah, but —

MARIE
And don't start up again on how his old man used to beat up on him all a time or his Mommy whored round with his uncle, or any of that crap, cause it ain't your problem.

FERN
That's not what I was gonna say.

MARIE
Look, you wouldn't listen to me back then when he was beatin' up on you, but I was right, right? And I'm right again now. Aid wouldn't dream of givin' a kid to a bum like Joe.

FERN

I just gets ascared when I thinks 'bout them takin' way my kids.

MARIE

I know. But who says they's gonna try and take your kids?

FERN

When they comes round I don't know what a say no more. What they wanna hear? What'll make them leave me alone?

MARIE

You just got a go 'long with them. You got a do what they wants.

FERN

Bunch a assholes. I hate them so much. I just hate them. I's so sick a them comin' round and tellin' me what to do. I tell you what the new worker says to me? You won't fuckin' believe this. "We's underpaid," she says. I'm cookin' a No Frills Kraft Dinner and she's drivin' a car, and she tells me she don't make enough money. I's so mad I wanna punch her out.

MARIE

You got a go 'long with them. You never gonna learn that? You got a do what they wants.

FERN

Just 'cause you don't mind havin' some old bitch asshole pokin' her nose round this place —

MARIE

Don't be stupid. I don't like it no more than you. What kind a fool you thinks I am? But that don't mean I ain't nice as pie when they's over. Took me a long time to learn it, Fernie, and I learned it a hard way sometimes.

FERN

Oh, sure.

MARIE   If you'd listen once in a while ya might save yourself a whole pile a trouble.

FERN   What a you knows?

MARIE   I know more than you.

FERN   Yeah, sure, you're so fuckin' smart.

MARIE   Can't tell you nothin', you knows it all. Miss Smarty Pants Herself. How many kids I had?

FERN   What?

MARIE   You're so goddam smart, how many kids I had?

FERN   What a you means?

MARIE   What's it sound like I mean? Simple question, ain't it? How many kids I had?

FERN   Two.

MARIE   Three!

FERN   Three? When?

MARIE   The time I went to Saint John with crazy Aunt Marsha.

FERN   The time you stay with her 'cause she's sick?

MARIE   No, fool. She ain't sick. 'Cept in her head. I was there cause Terry Doucette got me knocked up.

FERN   Ti-Puss Doucette's big brother? I never knows that.

MARIE   You was just a baby.

FERN   But nobody told me afters.

MARIE   You think Mom's gonna broadcast her daughter's a tramp?

FERN   So what happen?

MARIE   You knows how Aunt Marsha hates Frenchmen. She treat me like dirt.

            I had a little baby girl.

FERN   Yeah?

MARIE   Yeah. Day after St. Patrick's Day, about five in the morning. I seen her too, just after she's born. I wasn't gonna look at her, ya know, 'cause Aunt Marsha made me promise not to. She said if I didn't see her, I won't love her, and I ain't allowed to love her. So I kept my eyes closed all a time. But when I hear her cryin' and nurses sayin' she's a little girl, I got a see her, so I look and she's all red and wet ... They took her 'way for adoption somewheres.

FERN   Where?

MARIE   I don't know. She's a big girl now. Maybe in a high school somewheres.

FERN   Shit, Marie.

MARIE   Fernie, I seen her just a couple a seconds. I never even hold her in my hands. But she's mine and I still cries like a big baby sometimes

48

on her birthday. I couldn't do nothin' but give her up. Cripes, I just turn thirteen that March. I know she weren't really mine. But I still thinks about her.

So what'll I be like if they take away my boys? I knows them like the back a my hands. They take Mike and Bradley and puts them in a foster home, I'd go crazy. I'd end up crazy like old Jane Murray ya know, walkin' up and down Queen St. in a parka all summer, walkin' up and down like a retard lady talkin' to dead peoples.

FERN   Jesus ...

MARIE   So when my workers come by and says "Jump Marie!" I says "How high?" But they don't fool me. I ain't jumpin' for them, I's jumpin for my two kids. And I'd jump off the fuckin' moon!

You just got a let them think you're doin' what they wants.

FERN   But what I do with Joey? How come he never listens to me? How come he runs all over and don't listen? Ain't like I never give him stuff. He's gettin' them Star Wars sneakers next cheque.

And I don't treat him bad. I loves my kid.

MARIE   I know ya loves little Joey.

FERN   Then why don't he love me? How come he don't listen to me? What's fuckin' wrong with him? Little Jenny's fine. Why can't he be like his sister?

MARIE   He's just a little boy.

FERN   He's real smart in school, but he's fightin' so much that I had to go to a meetin' with that stupid kindygarden teacher. She says that he says the "f" word ten times a day. Every kid in the whole world says the "f" word. Ain't my fault that Joey says the fuckin "f" word. She makes me sick.

MARIE   Look, you just got a make like you're all upset and promise that Joey won't say it no mores.

FERN   I wish he's still a little baby sometimes. He was the prettiest baby I ever seen. 'Member? 'Member that nice nurse? She said so too. She said he was like a little angel, good as gold.

MARIE   He was a real good baby.

FERN   And people's so nice to me when he was little, ya know? I loved him so much then. I didn't even miss Joe when he left me.

MARIE   Aw forgets him, will ya! Jeez.

FERN   Fuck, Marie, Joe don't even live nowheres now. Sleeps at the mission or out a doors.

MARIE   He ain't your friggin' problem! Listen to me! I know them bums. Make ya feel all hot so ya think they mean somethin'. Worse'n that, ya thinks ya means somethin' to them.

FERN   But he —

MARIE   Oh, listen to me, will ya! Y'ain't fifteen no

mores. You can't go out to some tavern and find some horny bum to take ya home. Jeezo Cripes look at ya Fernie. Y'ain't even sure who was Jenny's father!

FERN   I's so sure. I knows too.

MARIE   Yeah, two or three, or four. Cripes, all you knows that he's white and not one a them wild Jamaicans ya ran 'round with.

Well, ya gots what you always said ya wants. Ya got your kids. Now ya got a forgets all 'bout bums like Joe. Ya got two little kids growin' up. Ya got a forgets about that hole between your legs.

FERN   Maybe the fuckin' Aid should take him. He don't listen to me. He's not like us, more like his old man every day. Actin' up like a little bum.

MARIE   Quit talkin' crazy. You don't give up on little Joey just cause he's actin' up.

FERN   It ain't no fairs. It ain't no fairs they got a grow up.

Scene Twelve

[FERN*'s kitchen, two years ago. A rainy afternoon. FERN is making sandwiches. JOEY is lying on the floor.*]

JOEY   Knock knock. Knock knock. I said "Knock knock."

[FERN *gives him a "gimme a break" look.*]

JOEY   *(Deep voice)* Who's there? *(Own voice)* Elvis
          Presley's underwear. *(Giggles)* Mommy? What's
          your name?

FERN   Mommy.

JOEY   And Mommy, Mommy, what's this? *(Points to
          his nose)*

FERN   Your nose.

JOEY   *(Holding out his hand)* And what've I got in my
          hand?

FERN   Nothin'.

JOEY   Mommy Nose Nothin.' Get it? Get it? Good
          joke, eh?

          [JOEY *rolls under the table.*]

FERN   What're you doin' now?

JOEY   I'm bored.

FERN   We can eat lunch soon.

JOEY   *(Groans)* It's boring here. Boring, boring, shitty
          and boring.

FERN   Quit that. I'm gonna send you to a new school.
          You swear too much there.

JOEY   Mommy?

FERN   Yeah?

JOEY   Knock knock.

FERN   Aw, no more jokes, eh?

JOEY   Just one.

FERN   Lunch is almost ready.

JOEY   I ain't hungry.

FERN   You said you wanted a sandwich.

JOEY   Oh. Take me to McDonald's.

FERN   Don't start that.

JOEY   I wanna go to McDonald's.

FERN   I made you the sandwich, now come and eat it.

JOEY   Make me.

FERN   Come here and eat it.

JOEY   No way, José.

FERN   If ya don't eat this sandwich, I'll give you a lickin'.

JOEY   Just try it.

FERN   Hey, Joey, don't do this to Mommy.

          [JOEY *rolls away from her.*]

FERN   Peanut butter's a new kind. Like on the cartoon shows.

JOEY   So?

FERN   You wanted me to get some for ya.

JOEY   So?

FERN   Aw, baby, I told that new worker you'd eat breakfast and lunch everyday now.

JOEY   I don't care.

FERN   I'm gonna give you the wooden spoon.

JOEY   No way, José.

FERN   Wait'll I catch ya!

[*She runs to him. He gets up but she catches him and sits on his stomach.*]

FERN   Gotcha!

JOEY   Lemme up.

FERN   No way, José.

JOEY   C'mon.

[*He struggles.*]

FERN   How you like this, eh?

[*She tickles him.*]

JOEY   Stop! Mommy stop!

FERN   Hungry yet? Eh eh?

JOEY   No nono no no no.

                [FERN *stops tickling him. He lies still.*]

FERN   Come and eat.

                [FERN *gets up, goes back to the table.*]

FERN   Now come and eat.

JOEY   Nope.

FERN   No more games. Come on.

JOEY   Catch me.

FERN   Quit it.

JOEY   *(Chants)* You can't catch me, you can't catch me.

FERN   I just caught you now come and eat 'fore I get
                real mad.

                [JOEY *starts running around and around.*]

JOEY   *(Chants)* Mommy's it
                Suck a tit
                Can't jump over a pile of shit!
                Mommy's it —

FERN   *(Blowing up)* QUIT IT!

JOEY   Suck a tit
                Can't jump over a pile of shit

                [*Lights begin to fade.*]

FERN   Come here!

[*Blackout. A slap.*]

SCENE THIRTEEN

[MARIE, *alone.*]

MARIE   One day all five a Mom's brothers come over
              from the Island on Uncle Al's fishin' boat. One
              a them summers when Dad took off. We all
              went down to the Point Wharf and they took us
              all for a ride. We's just jammed in there like a
              bunch a sardines. Jeez. Mom and her brothers
              and thirteen kids. No, twelve, cause Davey
              didn't wanna come. We had a picnic on a
              sandbar somewheres. You's maybe four,
              Sammy's just a little baby. Me and Gar went
              swimmin' and brung ya all these starfish and
              sand dollars we kept findin'. Jeez, I never seen a
              beach so loaded with them! And clams and
              quahogs, Cripes! Donna and Hen's diggin' them
              up all day ... Uncle Al took a tarp off a the boat
              and made a little lean-to for you to sit in out a
              the sun. Mom sticks you in it and says you
              looks just like the Queen of Sheeba on her high
              horse ... Mom and Uncle Al and Uncle Paul
              went for a long walk up the beach and you gots
              all mad when you couldn't go with'm. Y'always
              wanna be Mommy's little pet. I guess they's
              tryin' to figure out what to do 'bout Dad ... We
              played there all day long. When it's time to go
              back, Mom tells you to pick *one* starfish and *one*
              sand dollar cause there's just room for your
              favourites, and Jeezo Cripes, s'like she tried to
              kill you or somethin'! You starts screamin' and
              hollerin' "They's all my favourites, they's all my

favourites!" You just went crazy. So I pick out a couple a nice ones and took you back to the boat, and Donna sang ya them stupid cheatin' songs she's so crazy over. Bobby acted like a big show off to make you laugh and he fell off into the strait, almost got drownded. That's when Mom says, "Oh, just let that kid cry."... You's asleep when we got back to the Point that night. Mom offers to switch you for Sammy 'cause he's more little, but I says I'm big enough to carry you home from the shore piggy back. Everybody's cryin' and fightin' cause we's all so tired, and Mom tells us to quit it and think 'bout our uncles who got a take turns stayin' up and sailin' all night long to get home. And you starts talkin' in your sleep, Fernie, and we all stop and listen to ya and laugh and laugh without wakin' you up.

Then the moon comes out over the bay, and it's the biggest moon I ever seen in my whole life.

[*She smiles. Blackout.*]

SCENE FOURTEEN

[MARIE*'s apartment, a year and a half ago. A knock on the door. Another knock.*]

MARIE   *(Off)* Yeah, yeah, yeah.

[*Knock.*]

MARIE   *(Entering)* Hold your horses.

[FERN *and* FRED *open the door and come in. It is mid-afternoon and they have been drinking.*

FERN *giggles and hangs on to him. He wears a cowboy hat.*]

FERN   Hey, was you in the can or somethin'?

MARIE   No.

FERN   Well, where was ya?

MARIE   I was cleanin' up. Now what a you want?

FERN   Want you to meet my Freddy. Fred, this is Marie, my big sister.

FRED   I'm pleased to meet you, Marie.

[He puts out his hand, she ignores it.]

FERN   He's the one I told you 'bout.

MARIE   Right. Hi Freddy.

FRED   Pleased to meet ya. Your sister here talks about you a lot.

MARIE   I bet.

FERN   Ain't he cute?

MARIE   Look, I's sorry but —

FERN   Oh, we ain't stayin'. We just comes to say hello and have a beers with ya.

MARIE   I's out a beer.

FERN   Aw …

MARIE   Look —

FERN   C'mon, Marie, there's always beers here. Lemme
             check.

MARIE   Fernie!

FRED   Hey, Fern, maybe —

FERN   There's always beers here.

MARIE   You can't stay.

FERN   Oh?

MARIE   No, not today.

FERN   So who is you all a sudden?

MARIE   My worker's comin' over here any time now and
             I don't want her to find us all sittin' 'round here
             drunk.

FERN   Who says anythin' bout a drunk?

FRED   Just a friendly drink, Marie.

MARIE   Lookit, my kid's home from school soon, and
             my worker's comin' over here and I ain't about
             to have Happy Hour in my place.

FERN   Just one beer. Jeez. One little beer won't hurt.
             Freddy and me'll split it. Then we'll tell you the
             good news.

MARIE   Fernie, I ain't got time today.

FRED   C'mon, Fern. I don't think your big sister's feeling too friendly today.

MARIE   I got enough trouble with the Aid without you's —

FERN   Oh, so now I's trouble.

MARIE   Look, I had enough. It ain't even suppertime yet and you's drunk.

FERN   Don't get mad, we's just celebratin'.

MARIE   I don't care what you's doin', you got a go.

FRED   Now, listen here, Marie, no need to go makin' mountains out a molehills.

MARIE   *(To Fern)* Lookit. Take this bum a yours and —

FERN   HEY!

FRED   Watch it!

MARIE   I don't need this, just —

FRED   Watch who you call names, sister!

FERN   Who's you callin' a bum?

FRED   Let's get out a here.

FERN   When my sister says she's sorry.

FRED   I don't give a sweet shit if she's sorry, let's blow this dump.

MARIE	I ain't sorry.
FERN	Say you're sorry to Fred.
MARIE	I ain't sorry so I ain't sayin' it.
FERN	Then I ain't never comin' back here.
MARIE	Promises, promises.
FRED	Come on!
FERN	We just come to tell you the good news.
MARIE	What's that? That you picked up another bum? I's so sick a that! I is so goddam sick a that!
FRED	Bye Fern.
FERN	Freddy, waits up!
MARIE	Go on!
FERN	But Marie, I'm gettin' married!
MARIE	Married! To him! Ha!
FRED	*(Pulling Fern to the door)* Listen, sister —
MARIE	Don't you "sister" me! Don't you dare!
FRED	If I weren't a man, I'd slap you silly, 'cause you sure ain't no kind a lady!
MARIE	Get out a my place! Get out! The both a you's.
FERN	You ain't comin' to my weddin' now!

MARIE	GET OUT A HERE!
FERN	NOT IF YA GETS DOWN ON YOUR FUCKIN' KNEES AND BEGS ME, I WON'T LET YA COME!
MARIE	GET OUT!

[*Blackout.*]

SCENE FIFTEEN

[FERN*'s apartment, a year and a half ago. Morning. JOEY comes out of his bedroom door. He goes to the table, takes the top off the salt shaker and dumps salt into the sugar bowl. He exits. FERN comes out the other bedroom door in a housecoat and starts making two cups of instant coffee. FRED enters behind her a few moments later. He's wearing a bathrobe and cowboy boots. She looks into the children's room.*]

FERN	Bet he didn't eat no cereal. If he'd start eatin' that crap, worker'd get off my fuckin' back.
FRED	I wish you'd quit that swearin'.
FERN	I knows, I'm sorry, Freddy.
FRED	I don't wanna hear you talk dirty. You're too good for that.
FERN	I knows it's a bad way to talk.
FRED	I can hardly take it in a man, Fern, and I don't wanna hear it comin' from the girl I'm gonna marry.

62

FERN   I'm tryin' to quits it, okay?

FRED   *(Beat)* Kid didn't even say good-bye?

FERN   You hear'm?

FRED   No.

FERN   Then he didn't, did he?

FRED   I was just askin' a question.

FERN   I knows. Sorry.

FRED   *(Beat)* I tell you who I saw yesterday?

FERN   Who?

FRED   Over at Moss Park. With a bag a glue in his face. Can you guess?

[FERN *shrugs.*]

FRED   Old buddy a yours. I watched him pass right out on the grass. Kids playin' soccer come by and used him for a goal post. Him and a trash can.

FERN   Fred, quit it.

FRED   I was sittin' there thinkin' "What a born loser — "

FERN   Alright —

FRED   "What did my Fern ever see in that dope?" *(Beat)* "Like Father, like — "

FERN   Stop it! Just quit it!

FRED   I was only talkin' bout what I saw in Moss
            Park yesterday afternoon when you kicked me
            out a here.

FERN   You know fuckin' well that I didn't kick you out
            a here and that we'd both be up Shit's Creek if
            you's here when my worker comes 'round. And
            quit it on Joe.

            [*She gives him a coffee, and he puts sugar in it.*]

FERN   If the Housin' ever finds out you lives here —

            [FRED *sips and spits out a mouthful of coffee.*]

FRED   Jesus shit!

FERN   What's the matter?

FRED   You tryin' to kill me now?

FERN   What's wrong?

FRED   What's wrong? Taste it. Full a goddam salt.

            [*He tastes the sugar in the bowl.*]

FRED   It's that goddam kid.

FERN   Proves it.

FRED   You put salt in there?

FERN   Course I didn't.

FRED   Well then, who did? The baby? I know I sure as hell didn't.

FERN   Probably just made a mistake.

FRED   Don't cover up for him, you spoil that kid. He's a boy needs discipline.

FERN   Freddy —

FRED   What can you expect when his old man's a glue sniffin' loser?

FERN   Don't start it!

FRED   I ain't startin' nothin', baby. But you got a quit hidin' from facts.

FERN   I ain't hidin' from no facts. Okay?

FRED   *(Beat)* A little discipline never hurt anybody.

FERN   Lookit, you's hidin' right in there *(points to bedroom)* and listenin' when my worker says she's gonna call the cops if I hit'm anymores.

FRED   I never said a thing about hittin' him. More than one way to teach him a lesson.

FERN   We been all through this, Fred.

[*Pause. She starts to get him another coffee.*]

FRED   You mad?

FERN   No.

FRED   Wanna make up? Say we're sorry, kiss and make up? Wanna give me a little wet one?

FERN   Not now.

FRED   C'mon.

FERN   No.

FRED   Aw, hey. Not even a little one before the baby's up?

FERN   No. I don't feel like it.

FRED   C'mon. You always feel like it.

FERN   Oh yeah? Says who?

FRED   Says me. *(Pats his crotch)* And my Old Buddy says so too.

FERN   Oh, Jeez ...

FRED   Doncha pal? *(Rubs his crotch)* I was talkin' to my Old Buddy just this morning.

FERN   Oh, you was.

FRED   Yeah, I was. And he says you likes it so much there ain't enough hours in a day. Old Buddy says he figures you like him more'n you like me.

FERN   Yeah?

FRED   That's right. Only reason you keep Freddy around's for his Buddy.

FERN   That's what he said?

FRED   So help me God.

FERN   Just what I fuckin' needs — a man with a talkin' prick.

        [*Pause.*]

FRED   So what do you say? What do you say?

FERN   Oh, you talkin' to me?

FRED   Course I'm talkin' to you.

FERN   Oh. I thought maybe you was still talkin' to your dick.

FRED   You lookin' for a fight?

FERN   No. You?

FRED   Not in particular.

FERN   Then we won't fight.

FRED   Fine by me.

        [*Pause.*]

FRED   Coffee ready?

FERN   Yeah. How many cups you want?

FRED   Huh?

FERN   I said, how many cups you want, one or two?

FRED   What you mean?

FERN   Doesn't your fuckin' dink want a cup a coffee?

FRED   Quit that dirty talk! Come here!

            [*They stare at each other. She doesn't move. Then he grabs her, shoves her against the table and starts kissing her. Blackout.*]

            SCENE SIXTEEN

            [*A Welfare office.* FERN *and* ANNA *sit beside each other facing the audience.* FERN *looks haggard, tired.* ANNA *is a large woman in a sloppy black dress. They sit for a moment.*]

ANNA   What time's your appointment?

FERN   Ten.

ANNA   Comin' here to Welfare's gettin' as bad as going to the doctor's. They all double book. How many kids you got?

FERN   Um, two. A boy and a little girl name Jenny.

ANNA   I got five. Five. And they're all bad. They drive me crazy.

FERN   My boy's bad sometimes. I got a hard time make'm mind me.

ANNA   All of mine are bad. They never mind me. Well, my oldest girl's not so bad. She cooks and gets the others off to school. She's handy. I can't hardly seem to get up in the mornings. She

	really is a good kid to me. Sometimes I feel like she's my sister, except my sister and I never did get along. My name is Anna.
FERN	Fern.
ANNA	Fern. My, that's a pretty name. I like flower names. I almost named one girl Daisy, but her father wouldn't let me. Said it reminded him of Dagwood's dog, so we called her something else. That's my second oldest girl, my Lillian.
FERN	Oh. How old's the oldest?
ANNA	Fifteen. And I'm worried. Last thing I need's for her to go and get pregnant. I want her to wait until she's older or until she gets married. Besides, I don't know how I could get along without her. My kids are so bad and I feel sick most of the time.
FERN	That's too bad.
ANNA	Well, I'm used to sickness. Mother is a sick person and I take after her side. I had major surgery last month. In fact, there was still some blood in with my stool this morning. I should have cancelled this appointment. I've lost a terrible lot of weight and my doctors said it was a miracle of modern medicine that I did not die. That would have shown them.
FERN	Who?
ANNA	My bad kids. Where'd they be without their mother to put up with them? And whenever I tell them that, they just laugh at me. Kids have no

idea how hard they are to bring up. And let me tell you something. I've had "help" from the Children's Aid, and from the hospital, and from Social Services, and my kids have been tested at the Institutes, and put in special classes at school, and one of them was in a special school for awhile there because he was diagnosed as criminally insane when he was five, and do you know what all those educated people and agencies taught me?

[FERN *shakes her head.*]

That there's no substitute for a mother's love. They've all tried, the whole bunch of them, but they can't ever replace me, and that is something for you to remember always. I got this plaque up in the kitchen that says, "God Couldn't Be Everywhere So He Made Mothers." And that is God's Truth. So no matter what they tell you in here, you always remember that. It's in the Bible.

FERN   Aid's got a homemaker in now cause my boy's so bad.

ANNA   Well, you just remember that God Couldn't Be Everywhere So He Made Mothers.

FERN   Yeah, I —

ANNA   I just wish my bad kids would. They've taken to giving me presents.

FERN   That's nice.

[ANNA *glares at her.*]

Ain't it?

70

ANNA   Well, it's the presents. My boys Einstein and Cary made this doghouse at club. And they know we don't have and never will have a dog. Cats, yes. We have lovely cats. And they always have the best kittens in my building. Einstein and I had a terrible fight when I said there was no room in my bedroom for a doghouse. Then Cary brings home this plant stand he made me, and he knows how I hate plants. I'm no good with plants, I just kill them with kindness, and, besides, the kitties just paw them up and use them for litter boxes. So if I do something right and don't kill the plants, the cats get them anyways. And, anyways, they just stink with all that kitty do-do. *And* to add insult to injury, my little Lillian made this macrame plant hanger this big *(gestures huge with her arms)*. Well, this was right after Cary's plant stand fiasco and I got real mad. "Lillian." I says to her, "What am I supposed to put in this? It's big enough for a hedge!" So she had to cry and make a big fuss. They just don't realize! And Ford — he's my youngest and I spoil him — he remembered my birthday — which I try to forget 'cause there's not a thing as depressing as time passin' you by and, anyways, the doctors had me on enough valium to sedate a horse — and Ford he walks right into my bedroom with a card he made me about the size of a newspaper and starts crying when I won't pin it on the fridge. It wouldn't fit even if I tried! And his present he made me is a painting — "Art" they call it at school — and it's real messy and you couldn't tell what it was if you tried. Now, I love little Fordie, but he is *not* talented. And I don't understand why they make him do that at school. When will he ever get to use that the way he could use arithmetic or those things we got when we was kids. I make no bones about being old fashioned and believing firmly in the three R's.

FERN   What're they?

ANNA   Why Reading, Writing and Rithmetic.

FERN   Oh. Sometimes I wish I'd a finish school.

ANNA   That's a darn shame. But even my oldest has started with these presents. Even my Olive. She took up Shop just to spite me and she made me a dustpan. Now, I have a perfectly good yellow dustpan that I bought at Honest Ed's years ago and I know that she made this ugly thing out of tin just because I've been too sick to do the housework. Olive has started with these nasty presents now, too.

FERN   Aw ...

ANNA   And they all got together at Christmas and gave me the Pay TV just so they could watch dirty movies half the night, and now I have to pay the bills every month! I tell you, without a mother's love those kids would be out in the street. Hardly even makes the Baby Bonus worth while, now does it? I mean, when you really think about it, why do we work hard to bring them up good? But where would they be without us? No, let me tell you something. There's all these people, like this bunch here at the Welfare, who tell you what you should do and how you should bring up your kids and all that other stuff they take in fancy colleges. Half of them don't have kids. They never will. But where are they when you're feeling sick as can be and your kid walks in with a goddam doghouse? No. God Couldn't Be Everywhere So He Made Mothers. That is what is called a proverb and I run my life by it. If I didn't believe it, I'd walk right out in front of a fast car.

[*Blackout.*]

SCENE SEVENTEEN

[FERN's *apartment. Darkness.*]

FRED'S VOICE   You don't know what lovin' is till you've spent forty-eight hours solid in a motel unit.

[FRED *lights a cigarette.*]

FRED   More private than here. Once that door's shut no one can bug ya. And their sheets so white they shine on after you turn out the lights.

[FERN *lights a cigarette. Lights come up slowly. It is very late at night.* FERN *and* FRED *have been making love.*]

FRED   Ya just close that door, strip down to nothin', and get to it. Order in pizza and eat it stark naked in the bath tub. How's that sound?

FERN   Expensive.

FRED   J'ever do it standin' up in one a them tin motel room showers? With the water runnin'? Slippin' and slidin' around. Wet outside as y'are in. I wanna tell ya, it's the closest thing to the way they do it in Heaven.

FERN   Heaven!

FRED   Yeah, Heaven. Flyin' around them big clouds, doin' it forever and ever amen!

FERN   I know why I loves you *(Giggles)*.

FRED   Cause I got stayin' power.

FERN   No, cause you're so full a shit. Screwin' in Heaven. Jeezo, Freddy.

FRED   You think I won't be able to touch you up there?

FERN   Only part to touch in Heaven'll be my soul.

FRED   Then my soul'll come swoopin' down and bang ya silly.

FERN   Souls don't got no dinks.

FRED   Oh no?

FERN   No. If you's a soul you'd look like Barbie doll's boyfriend Ken. Just a little lump a stupid plastic 'tween your legs, good for nothin'. That's why they never got married, had no kids.

FRED   Who?

FERN   Barbie and Ken.

FRED   'Cept I got more'n some old rubber doll, hey? I got my Old Buddy here.

FERN   You and your Old Buddy.

74

FRED	He likes my Heaven better'n yours, doncha pal? Hey Fern, let's just fuck forever and order in.

[*He begins to make love to her.*]

FERN   *(Gently)* Aw, Freddy.

FRED   What?

FERN   Can't we just be quiet awhiles, okay?

FRED   Aw, come on, Fern. Your kids can't bug us now.

FERN   Jeez …

FRED   C'mon, babe.

FERN   There nothin' else y'ever think of?

FRED   I like to eat.

FERN   Big surprise. F'you could gets a job *eatin'*, me and the kids'd be livin' like millionaires.

[*Pause.*]

FRED   Well?

FERN   Well what?

FRED   What're you gettin' at?

FERN   Nothin'.

FRED   Oh, yeah?

FERN   Hey, let's just quit it 'fore we even starts.

FRED   Quit what?

FERN   Quit startin' fightin', okay?

FRED   I ain't startin' nothin'.

[*He moves slightly away.*]

FERN   *(Tenderly)* Freddy?... Freddy?

FRED   What?

FERN   What're we gonna do?

FRED   Well, it looks like we ain't gonna fuck no more.

FERN   I don't mean now. You know what I mean. What's I gonna do with Joey?

[*He doesn't respond.*]

He took off this mornin' at recess time. Run aways from school. Went to Allen Gardens all day. He's talkin' all day to some guy workin' there. Told'm he's a orphan. Says a car crash killed all a his family and he lives with a mean old witch. Tells lies all day long to some guy workin' in Allen Gardens. He just lies and lies like a little liar. Then that garden guy calls the cops, cops call the Aid, Aid calls my worker, worker gimme shit. Worker asked me questions 'bout you.

FRED   How's she know about me?

FERN   They knows 'bout everything.

FRED   How?

FERN   They just does.

FRED   What she wanna know?

FERN   If we got plans. Weddin' plans or anythin'.

FRED   None a her goddam business.

FERN   She says anythin' to do with kids *is* her business.

FRED   Well, you just tell her I ain't got nothin' to do with kids. Tell her Freddy is Adults Only. *(Touches her)* I'm the part of your life that's Restricted, hey? Got a be eighteen.

FERN   *(Touches his hand)* What're we gonna do? Freddy?

            [*Pause.*]

FRED   Well, I know what I'm gonna do soon.

FERN   What's that?

FRED   I'm goin' back to B.C.

FERN   Oh ...

FRED   I've been thinkin'.

FERN   Well, you quits thinkin'.

FRED   No, there's work for me there. I can get work with my brother in Cranbrook. I can start makin' big dollars.

            [*Pause.*]

FERN   You'd just leave me?

FRED   I can't stay here, Honey. I ain't no big city boy.
        C'mon Fern, there ain't no work and that dopey
        sister a yours treats me like trash. I got a get out
        a here ... Look, I wanna go home where there's
        work for me.

FERN   You can't leave me, Freddy.

FRED   Know what I am to you?

FERN   What?

FRED   T-R-O-U-B-L-E.

FERN   What's that?

FRED   Trouble. I spell trouble.

FERN   Oh Freddy, no ya don't. Don't say that. You's the
        only thing that ain't trouble. You's the only
        thing that makes me feel good anymores.

FRED   Yeah?

FERN   Yeah. I'd go crazy without you. I gets ascared.

FRED   Scared a what?

FERN   I donno — everything. (Beat) You's away all
        day today and when I didn't know where you
        was, it's like when I was little. Like when
        Donna'd find me hidin' in the old trunk in the
        shed and she'd shut the top and sit on it.
        Know that kind a scared? That's me without
        you.

78

[FRED *caresses her.*]

Oh, baby, I's so worried 'bout where you's gone, I just stand there by the window. Jenny was cryin' and cryin' and I goes in and tells her to quiet up, but she just gets louder and drives me crazy and I slaps her. And she's louder and louder and I slaps her more. Then I hear it's me cryin' real loud, and I gets ascared and quits hittin'r. I hold'r real tight and kiss'r and kiss'r and sings a little, and she stops cryin' and goes to sleep. And I miss you so much! I think what'll I do if you leaves me? What if it's just me alone with the kids? Then cops come with Joey, and the worker shows up and gimme shit. Then Joey starts runnin' round and runnin' round and he won't eat nothin' I try and fix for supper, and he starts Jenny cryin' again. I ask him why he tells that guy I's dead in a car crash, and he just starts laughin' and makin' faces and he takes off.

You won't leave me, will ya Freddy? You can't leave me alone with the kids. Don't leave me. Hold onto me.

[*He holds her.*]

FRED   Aw, now. C'mon, baby. S'okay. *(Kisses her face)* Hey? Your Freddy's here. *(Kisses her)* Hey? Where's my old Fern?... That's better. Yeah. *(Kiss)* You know, I wanted to have you that first second I saw you walk into that tavern.

FERN   Yeah?

FRED   You betcha. Soon's that waiter told you to get

out and you grabbed his tray and pitched it ...
I knew. *(Grins)* Woo! You were somethin',
Fern baby.

FERN   Yeah?

FRED   Yeah. I'd've been a big damn fool not to run
after you. But I caught up with ya, hey?

FERN   And you won't go way now, will ya?

[*Pause.*]

FRED   J'ever see mountains, Fern? Not dopey hills like
ya got back east, but big mountains made out a
rocks?

FERN   Oh, Freddy, no.

FRED   Why don't ya come out west with me, Fern? Be
the first vacation y'ever had in your life I bet.
We can just jump into the car, head out, and hit
every motel unit from here to the Rocky
Mountains. Hey? How about that? Turn that
old car a mine into a travellin' sex machine, hey?
Love on wheels. I've been waitin' for someone
like you for so long.

FERN   Oh, Freddy ...

FRED   C'mon, baby.

FERN   But my kids.

FRED   You need to get away from those kids a yours.

FERN   What a ya means?

FRED	Just what I said. You need a break. Get that sister a yours to take them.
FERN	Marie? No way. She wouldn't anyways.
FRED	Call the worker then.
FERN	The worker?
FRED	Yeah. She says anythin' to do with kids is her business — let her figure it out.
FERN	What a ya mean? Freddy?
FRED	Leave'm. C'mon baby.

SCENE EIGHTEEN

[*Music fades in, "Rubber Dolly." Lights up on* JOEY *in his space. He sits up and begins playing with his jacket. He wears it like a cape and poses like Superman. He pretends to be a bullfighter. He drapes it over his head and walks like a monster. The music gives way to the sound of a train. The* SAILOR *appears in dim light by the train door.*]

SAILOR	Baby, over here. C'mere. Yeah.

[FERN *goes to the* SAILOR. *They embrace.*]

FERN	Maybe somebody sees us?
SAILOR	Naw, this train's asleep. That feel good? [*He touches her. They kiss. The* SAILOR *starts to make love to her, very brusquely, emotionless.* FERN *begins kissing his face, his neck, but he*

doesn't respond to her kisses. He fumbles with their clothing. He begins moving his hips. The train noises are louder, wilder.]

FERN   Baby, oh ... so much, so much ...

SAILOR   Un! Un!

FERN   I love you so much!

                [FERN *looks over the* SAILOR's *back and sees* JOEY.]

FERN   Oh, baby.... Stop, baby, stop!

                [*She tries to struggle free from the* SAILOR, *but he holds her tightly. Train noises are louder, more discordant.*]

FERN   Stop it! Leave me! Lemme go! Get your coat! Lemme go! Stop it baby!

                [*She and* JOEY *watch each other. A moment. Blackout. Train sounds fade into the distance.*]

FERN'S VOICE   Joey! Jenny! Joooey! Marie! Marie!

                SCENE NINETEEN

                [FERN *and* MARIE]

FERN   You got a come with me, Marie.

MARIE   No, I don't. I don't got a do nothin' with you. I don't want nothin' to do with you.

FERN   But you's my sister, and flesh and blood.

MARIE   And your kids's flesh and blood too, but ya gives
          them up for a bum. You don't got no kind a
          blood I understand.

FERN   I got a get them back!

MARIE   Weren't two weeks ago when you's standin' right
          there tellin' me you got a gives them up. Jeezo.
          "They's makin' me crazy, Marie, I gots to get
          aways." Cripes, make up your mind.

FERN   I made up my mind — come and help me get
          my kids back. Please.

MARIE   Maybe Aid should keep your kids.

FERN   Marie!

MARIE   Never thought I'd hear the likes a that come out
          a my mouth, but Jeezo, I never heard a nobody
          who'd dump her own two kids in a foster home
          some she could take off halfways to China with
          some joy ridin' bum

FERN   But I come back, didn't I?

MARIE   No big surprise to me you's back with your tail
          between your legs. I knows that kind a bum.
          You think I never made a fool of myself over
          some bum like Fred? But I didn't throw my kids
          away.

FERN   You got a help me tell'm why they got a give me
          my kids back. I'll just get mad and I won't be
          able to make it sound right. You got a help me
          do it right.

MARIE	Who says? Who says I got a?" Lookit here, Fernie, it ain't my problem. I got my own problems and you ain't one a them. I got a kid failin' school. I got a kid picked up by the cops.
FERN	Marie, if I don't get'm back, I go crazy.
MARIE	So what? Last week if you don't give'm up you'll go crazy.
FERN	Please Marie!
MARIE	I can't take it no mores, Fernie. Jeez, all y'ever do anymore is break my fuckin' heart. You's always so stupid actin' and talkin' big. Why didn't ya ever listen? Why didn't ya listen to me just one time?
FERN	What I got a do? Get down on my fuckin' knees and beg and says I's sorry ten hundred million times? If that's what ya want, I'll do it, I'll do anything.
MARIE	S'no good, Fernie. That day when you give up your kids, I gives up on you. I just gives up.
FERN	Don't! I's sorry. You's right, you's always right. I's stupid. I's sorry.
MARIE	Aw, quit it! It's your sister you're talkin' to, not some dumb, fuckin' retard. Don't come beggin' 'round here just cause Fred beat up on ya.
FERN	That ain't why I's back. I come back for my kids. I come back to change everythin', make it all better. You got a helps me!

MARIE   I's sick and tired a helpin' you Fernie! I been doin' it since the day you was born.

FERN   But ya got a this time! It's different!

MARIE   Yeah? Ha!

FERN   I's through with Freds. Who needs me is my kids, and I was as mean to my kids as Mom was to me.

MARIE   Mom never run off, she never left ya, never.

FERN   She didn't have to go nowheres to leave me! Once I got borned she didn't give a sweet fuck and you knows it!

[MARIE *says nothing.*]

I knows now that Mom ain't never got love for me like I gots for Joey and Jenny.

MARIE   What makes you think your love's so special?

FERN   'Cause I feels it!

Fred and me's at some prairie gas station at night, and we's standin' by the pumps and fightin'. There was peoples there watchin' but they don't count. All that counts is my kids. And I starts screamin' at Fred, "I fuckin' dares ya to leave me here, I double dares ya." And that little asshole just jumps in his car and takes off.

MARIE   And leaves you standin' there like a little fool. Fuck, Fern.

FERN   I look at those assholes starin' at me, and I says, "Whyncha take a picture, it'll last longer!"

MARIE   Jeez. Y'acted like a goddam kid.

FERN   No. Right then I was somethin' big from a Sunday School story. I pass through them assholes and cross over that highway like one a them pillars a fire. All I's thinkin' is my kids. I's crossin' that Trans-Canada to hike back here and I feel all a my love comin' back into me like high tide. I start walkin' and I's so full a fuckin' love like I's just gonna blow up if I don't start movin' and screamin' out the names a my kids. Screamin' out "Jenny!", screamin' out "Joey!" Walkin' 'long there till a big silver truck comes to bring me home.

        You got a come help me, Marie! Those kids are waitin' for me!

SCENE TWENTY

[MARIE, *alone.*]

MARIE   Kids is fine. Mike and Jenny don't got nothin' to do with each other much, but that Bradley, ha, he sure love his little cousin. He takes her to the Day Cares and picks her up afters. I told'm a hundred times not to ride'r double on that crazy bike a his, but she just keeps askin' and he can't say no to her. She's just like you. I said to Mom on the phone last week that little Jenny even eats like you. 'Member how you used a make mountains out a your mash potatoes and drive us all crazy? She's your kid alright. When she's havin' a big tantrum I just roll'r up in a blanket and hold'r tight and rock'r till she's all better. She's my little angel.

SCENE TWENTY-ONE

[FERN *and* JOEY.]

FERN
Joey, c'mon! I already took your sister 'cross the hall and I promise the teachers ya wouldn't be late no mores.

C'mon.

[JOEY *is playing with a Masters of the Universe He Man doll.*]

JOEY
Yeah, yeah.

FERN
C'mon. Teacher said you's doin' good in school.

JOEY
You know what? Me and Josh built a fort!

FERN
Yeah? You know there's no black kids when I was little? I never seen no black people when I was a kid. I never seen a real one till I come to Toronto. Just pictures.

JOEY
How come?

FERN
There weren't none.

JOEY
Where was they?

FERN
They was here, maybe. Or Jamaica. And there's no Chinamans neither where I growed up.

JOEY   Grew up.

FERN   Just white people. There was English and French white people.

JOEY   We gots this new kid at school. He's from this new place called Louse.

FERN   Where's that? I ain't never heard a no place called Louse.

JOEY   There's a big war there. He seen it. And they had to throw pigs off the boats at night 'cause they was too noisy.

FERN   Yeah? Put on your coat.

JOEY   He's Chinese, sort a, he's funny. Can he come for supper?

FERN   No, not today.

JOEY   Tomorrow?

FERN   I don't know, now put on your coat.

JOEY   Why can't he come for supper?

FERN   'Cause I said so. Now, put on your coat. I promise the teacher you'd wear it everyday now.

JOEY   When can he come for supper?

FERN   Joey, don't ask me now, okay?

JOEY   No fair, you're mean.

FERN	Lookit, I'm tired. Just put on your coat, baby.
JOEY	No. I didn't have to wear no coat at the foster home.
FERN	I don't care 'bout what you did at no foster home.
JOEY	They was nice to me there. Better than you.
FERN	Quit it or I'll send you back.
JOEY	Good.
FERN	Just put on your coat, will you?
JOEY	They was nicer than you.
FERN	Put on your coat now!
JOEY	No! Make me!
FERN	Put on the coat!
JOEY	No way José.
FERN	Will you just put on the fuckin' coat!
JOEY	Ohoh, Mommy said the "f" word.
FERN	PUT IT ON NOW!
JOEY	You can't make me.
FERN	Quit it!
JOEY	They said you're bad.

FERN   *(Explodes)* PUT THAT THING ON OR I'LL HIT YA!

JOEY   *(Laughs)* You can't make me, you can't make me!

[FERN *tries to grab him, but he runs away from her.*]

JOEY   You can't catch me, you can't catch me!

FERN   STAND STILL, I'M GONNA GIVE YOU THE WOODEN SPOON!

JOEY   Na nana na naaaaa!

[JOEY *is still laughing when* FERN *grabs him. Blackout.*]

SCENE TWENTY-TWO

[FERN, *now. Alone.*]

FERN   I just want him to quit buggin' me. Teacher was mad at me 'cause I can't never make'm wears a coat. Wasn't till cops put me in a car in front a my buildin' and there was some guy there callin' at me with a fancy camera that I knows I was a killer for real. I always thought killers was the worst anybody'd ever be. Then it was that mornin' and I was gettin' into the cop car with that newspaper guy takin' my picture. I never thought I'd be in the papers ever. Now I think that them that saw me first time in the papers think I never loved my kids. And my kids think it, too. Little Joey's dead and he hates me. Nothin' else just don't matter. I know I'm lucky to be here and not in a jail 'cause they say I was

90

crazy, but it's all a same to me. I can't hardly looks at Jenny when they brings her to see me. She's ascared a my love. And I know Marie don't wanna let'm give'r back to me.

Sometimes I wanna be dead — like jumps out a window or somethin'? But when I thinks 'bout it I gets ascared that when I'm dead somewheres Joey'd be there, and he'd look at me, and I can't stand it. I think 'bout bein' with him and I gets crazy.

I makes stuff for Jenny. They's learnin' me to read so's I can tell'r stories, and I's makin' little doll clothes and stuff. I try and thinks 'bout gettin' her back, and me and her'd go and live in a pretty little house in a woods, all yellow or somethin'. With candies. I tries and thinks about it, but it can't too much cause it always turns out bad. And I start thinkin' 'bout what happened and how ascared he got all a sudden. He was buggin' me 'bout supper and buggin' me 'bout his coat and runnin' and runnin' round. He won't listen. He won't love me. He was laughin' and laughin' at me and then he was ascared all a sudden, and I was thinkin' "S'about time you stay in one place long enough to hear how much I loves ya!" And I can hear my love so loud it's screamin'. Then he was all blue.

I just want'm to know I love'm. But he ain't gonna believe that. Not never ever.

He ain't never gonna know how much I love him.

[*Fade to black.*]

Running Far Back

For JoAnna McIntyre

Cast

LORETTA ESTABROOKS
BOBBY ESTABROOKS, her brother
MILDRED ESTABROOKS, their mother
NORMAN ESTABROOKS, their father
BENOIT CHAISSON, Loretta's husband
MICKEY CHAISSON, Loretta and Benoit's son
JOSSETTE HEBERT

"RUNNING FAR BACK" is set on a beach in southeastern New Brunswick. The beach is not realistic, but it must have elements of the real and be adaptable for all scenes. Although there must be no cumbersome props and set pieces, there should be specific areas for the home in New Brunswick, the Dorchester Penitentiary, the apartment in Montreal, the beach itself, etc.

The events of the play span the early fifties to 1980, although Act One is centred around 1967 and Act Two, 1980. In 1967 Loretta is 15 and Bobby is 18 years old. {All scenes are dated with brackets.}

There are no blackouts between scenes. Unless indicated in the script, Bobby and Loretta are onstage throughout the play, and we are always aware of both ofthem.

"RUNNING FAR BACK" does not have a chronological time structure, however there is an emotional chronology for Bobby and Loretta. It is important that emotions from one scene carry over and overlap with the next.

An earlier, substantially different version of "RUNNING FAR BACK," entitled "LORETTA AND HER BROTHER," was produced for CBC Radio by Greg Sinclair. The radio script was published by Prentice Hall in Volume Two of their "3D English" series.

"Running Far Back" was first produced by the Great Canadian Theatre Company, Ottawa in November 1994 with the following cast:

Loretta	Kate Newby
Bobby	Thomas Bailey
Mildred	Kate Hurman
Norman	John Koensgen
Benoit	Benoit Osborne
Jossette	Danielle Desormeaux
Mickey	Ajay Fry

Sets and Costumes	Art Penson
Music	Ian Tamblyn
Stage Manager	Françine Lapointe

The play was directed by JoAnna McIntyre.

"Running Far Back" was workshopped at the Banff Playwrights Colony and at Canadian Stage in Toronto.

ACT ONE

SCENE ONE

The sound of the sea, soft and lulling, grows and fades under the first scene.

Dressed in a pair of flannel pyjamas, MICKEY, *age 6, is sleeping in his crib. He gets out of bed and walks in his sleep, dragging his little blanket {1980}. He walks past* BOBBY *and* LORETTA *as children — they are hiding in a pile of old canvas {1957}.* LORETTA *takes the blanket as it passes.*

BOBBY *tickles her sides, she laughs. While the scene with* LORETTA *takes place,* BENOIT *goes to* MICKEY, *picks him up and carries him back to his crib.*

BOBBY   Coochy coochy coochy coochy coochy coochy.

BENOIT   Mickey? Tu dors? Viens avec papa, viens te recoucher.

LORETTA   Quit it! Bobby! Quit it! They'll hear us. Stop it or I'll be sick! Tickle Man's for babies. I'm six years old now. I ain't a baby no more.

BOBBY   Yes you is, my little baby sister.

LORETTA   Bobby, they catch us, what'll we do?

BOBBY   They ain't gonna catch us. We just took some chips.

LORETTA   I shouldn't a had a smoke.

BOBBY   Ya wanted to.

LORETTA   Mrs. Bourgeois, she won't let us buy stuff in her store again ever. I'll hafta get Jossette to buy chips and pop for me.

BOBBY   Quiet, or I'll hafta tickle ya again.

LORETTA   No one's gonna let me inside anywhere no more. Mrs. Hebert won't let Jossette and Louis play with us again ever.

BOBBY   Tickle Man's comin'.

LORETTA   No Bobby no.

BOBBY   Yes Retta yes.

            [*He tickles her again.*]

BOBBY   Coochy coochy coochy coochy coochy coochy.

            [LORETTA *pushes him away.*]

LORETTA   Quit it!

            [*He stops tickling her, but he stays very close. They are lying together quietly.*
            BENOIT *is sitting beside* MICKEY *{1980}.*
            These two scenes dovetail.]

BOBBY   All better?

LORETTA   No. You're a mean brother, a big meanie.

[*He touches her stomach. The scene becomes sexual, not in a frightening way, first playful, then uncomfortable.*]

[*Lights stronger on* MICKEY *and his father.* BENOIT *touches* MICKEY's *stomach, chest, etc. as he says the rhyme. At the end he taps* MICKEY *on the forehead and they laugh.* BOBBY *touches* LORETTA *in the same places.*]

BENOIT — Estomac de plomb, — Gorge de pigeon, — Menton fourchu, — Goule d'argent, — Joue bouillie, — Joue routie, — Nez quinquin, — P'tit oeil, — Gros-t-oeil, — Poque la maillloche![1]

[BOBBY *kisses her.*]

MICKEY — Poque la maillloche!

[LORETTA *raises herself on her elbows, looks at* BENOIT *and* MICKEY. *She pushes* BOBBY *away.* MICKEY *is falling asleep.*]

LORETTA — Bobby I started school now. I ain't a baby, not no more.

[LORETTA *is an adult, no longer in the scene with* BOBBY. *She leaves* BOBBY *and goes to* BENOIT.]

BENOIT — My wife has the most beautiful bum in Eastern Canada.

[1] Lead stomach, - Pigeon breast, - Forked chin, - Silver mouth, - Boiled cheek, - Roasted cheek, - Funny little nose, - Little eye, - Big eye, - Beat the drum!

LORETTA   Don't talk like that.

BENOIT   He's asleep again.

[*He touches her bottom {1980}.*]

BENOIT   *(Whispers:)* It's so magnificent, I still want to —

[*She wriggles away.*]

LORETTA   No, Ben, no Benoit.

BENOIT   What's wrong?

LORETTA   Nothing. *(Beat)* I'm taking Mickey and going back home.

BENOIT   I'll come too.

LORETTA   No.

BENOIT   Why not?

LORETTA   Because I don't want you to.

BENOIT   Why not?

[*He moves towards her.*]

LORETTA   Don't touch me!

BOBBY   Retta?

BENOIT   What's the matter?

LORETTA   I'm getting out a here.

[*She walks away from him.*]

BENOIT Wait!

BOBBY Retta? Loretta?

[LORETTA *goes to* BOBBY.]

LORETTA You ruined everything. Everything!

[*A beat, then she shoves him off the canvas. She begins working at the canvas, turning it into a tent. The lights begin to fade to twilight.*]

[BOBBY *throws a sleeping bag at her.*]

LORETTA Hood!

[BOBBY *exits {1967}. Benoit* goes to MICKEY's *room where lights fade.* LORETTA *is alone. Night and stars.*]

SCENE TWO

[LORETTA *works on the tent. The sound of waves grows louder and, beneath it, the sound of boys shouting in the distance.* LORETTA *stands very still, listening. The shouting becomes louder, fighting. Wave sounds transform into the roar of a car with a Hollywood muffler. A police siren sounds over this and both fade into the distance. Waves sounds again, which fade under the scene {1967}.*
JOSSETTE *runs on with her radio blaring. Song is "World Without Love" by Peter and Gordon.*]

LORETTA Turn it down!

JOSSETTE   But it's live tonight from Dance-a-Rama.

LORETTA   We got a hear or Mom'll sneak up on us and catch us drinkin' and they won't let us sleep out no more all summer. Won't even think 'bout lettin' me go to Expo with ya.

JOSSETTE   Bite my head off why doncha.

LORETTA   So ya get some?

JOSSETTE   Yeah, finally. Stupid bootlegger must a asked about a million questions, but I just lied. Hey, there's somethin' happenin' down at the beach, just past the Blue Circle.

LORETTA   I know. Sounded like a fight. Help me with this, will ya?

            [Jossette *puts down the wine and helps* LORETTA *with the tent. Both girls are giddy, and their foolishness escalates throughout the scene.*]

JOSSETTE   I seen your dad there.

LORETTA   At the bootleggers? Oh, jeese.

JOSSETTE   But he didn't see me. He's out back havin' a drink with old Romeo. *(Beat)* I thought Bobby was gonna help with this.

LORETTA   Dream on.

JOSSETTE   Ya got a sleepin' bag for me?

LORETTA   Yeah, I got Bobby's.

JOSSETTE   Yeah? Ya think that was his car with a siren chasin' after it?

LORETTA   Serve'm right if he gets a speedin' ticket. Actin' big all a time. Thinks he invented how to spit for jeese sakes.

JOSSETTE   He's a hood.

LORETTA   He is not!

JOSSETTE   Ya said so yourself.

LORETTA   I never said my brother's a hood. Just 'cause he acts like a jerk don't mean he's a hood.

JOSSETTE   Ya said he stole that waterproof watch he give ya for Christmas.

LORETTA   I just said *maybe*. I might let ya wear it swimmin' tomorrow.

JOSSETTE   Yeah?

LORETTA   Maybe. Where's Louis tonight?

JOSSETTE   He tole Ti-Pop he's goin' for a walk or somethin'.

[*They finish the tent.*]

LORETTA   There, that's it.

JOSSETTE   Let's have a drink.

LORETTA   This wine need a corkscrew or anythin'?

JOSSETTE   A corkscrew? Jeese, I bought it from the bootlegger, not the friggin' King a France.

[*They drink.*]

LORETTA   Ja see Expo 67 on TV last night?

JOSSETTE   I asked my mudder again 'bout if ya can come wit us when we go, and she says ya could, maybe, 'cause there's extra beds at my Aunt Clemence, but there ain't room in the car so ya can't. If my stupid brother'd stay home, then ya could come. 'Cept that's where he wants to go to "university" so I don't think so.

LORETTA   My mom and I had a big fight bout it 'cause she said all Centennial Year is is a excuse to be stupid.

JOSSETTE   My mudder says that yours'd bitch about the Blessed Virgin if she came over.

LORETTA   She sure would — Virgin Mary's a Catholic.

JOSSETTE   Y'ever think it's funny us bein' best friends when our mudders get along so bad?

LORETTA   *(Beat)* Ya think Expo's really as good as they make it look on TV? Famous people are prob'ly there right now.

JOSSETTE   Famous people've been here.

LORETTA   Oh big deal. Kate Smith was here once on her way Overseas in World War Two. Some old fat lady on "Ed Sullivan," old enough to be dead.

JOSSETTE Only famous people ya'll see are dem Quebec singers Louis's so crazy bout.

LORETTA What's wrong with them?

JOSSETTE When you ever hear'm?

LORETTA Louis played some for me one time.

JOSSETTE When?

LORETTA Last month sometime.

JOSSETTE Where was I?

LORETTA I donno. In Moncton, maybe. Buyin' shoes.

JOSSETTE How come ya never told me?

LORETTA I donno. Ya never asked.

JOSSETTE You two goin' love mental or somethin'?

LORETTA No. *(Beat)* Don'tcha think he's cute?

JOSSETTE My brother? That's a hot one.

LORETTA If I tell ya somethin', promise ya won't laugh at me.

JOSSETTE What?

LORETTA Ya got a promise.

JOSSETTE Okay, I promise.

LORETTA No, really really promise.

JOSSETTE   Okay, okay, I promise I won't laugh at ya or it'll be a sin.

LORETTA   *(Beat)* I really like Louis.

JOSSETTE   Your kiddin'.

LORETTA   Swear to God. We talk about things, you know, we talk about things.

JOSSETTE   What things?

LORETTA   Like, about the war in Viet Nam, or Quebec, or movies.

JOSSETTE   Mr. Know It All.

LORETTA   Just cause he's interested in stuff, you guys all make fun a him. He's so quiet most a the time, but when I'm alone and talkin' to'm, he gets all excited bout stuff — *(Beat)* We talked bout what we'll do at Expo.

JOSSETTE   Big thrill. He'll drag ya off to hear one a them chanteuse all screamin' 'bout bein' broke up — gives me a pain.

LORETTA   Oh, come on, even you can see that he's not like the other jerks around here. I mean, even his hair's like somebody's from away. The way it comes down cross his forehead.

JOSSETTE   Jeese. You're more'n Love Mental. You're sick in the head.

[*A siren wails very loud and very close.*]

JOSSETTE   Cripes!

LORETTA   It's goin' down to the beach!

[*Another siren, followed closely by a third.*]

LORETTA   Cops and ambulance too.

JOSSETTE   And the Mounties!

MILDRED   *(Off)* Loretta?

LORETTA   S'my mom. Get rid a the wine, fast!

[*They take the wine into the tent.*]

LORETTA   You got a Cert or somethin'?

JOSSETTE   Eat some grass.

MILDRED   Loretta? Could you girls come here, please?

LORETTA   Whasamatter Mom?

[MILDRED *enters.*]

MILDRED   Retta, is Jossette there with you?

LORETTA   What do you want Mom?

MILDRED   I asked you to come here! Do it now!

LORETTA   Oh, okay.

[*The girls come out of the tent.*]

JOSSETTE   Hi Mrs. Estabrooks.

MILDRED   Hi Jossette.

LORETTA   What is it Mom?

MILDRED   Jossette, I think you'd better go home now.
           There's been some kind a trouble and you better
           go home till things get straightened up.

JOSSETTE   What trouble?

MILDRED   You better hurry home, your folks'll be lookin'
           for you.

JOSSETTE   Oh jeese, what is it?

MILDRED   Loretta, say good-bye to Jossette.

LORETTA   Mom, can't I walk her part way?

MILDRED   No!

JOSSETTE   It was my fault Mrs Estabrooks.

MILDRED   What?

JOSSETTE   I bought it, not Loretta.

LORETTA   Jossette!

MILDRED   Bought what?

JOSSETTE   The wine we was drinkin'.

MILDRED   What? Oh, Jossette girl, for godsakes just go
           home now.

JOSSETTE   Okay. Night.

LORETTA   I'll call ya tomorrow. We'll go swimmin'.

JOSSETTE   Night.

LORETTA   Night Jossette.

               [JOSSETTE *exits. The lights start to fade.*]

MILDRED   Get your stuff out a that tent and get inside the
               house this instant.

LORETTA   We hardly drank anythin', ya know.

MILDRED   Loretta Estabrooks!

LORETTA   Mom? What's goin' on?

               [*They start to exit.*]

MILDRED   Oh, Retta, somethin' real bad's happened.

LORETTA   What?

MILDRED   Jossette's brother Louis got himself killed in a
               fight down at the beach, and the cops is lookin'
               for Bobby.

LORETTA   Killed?

MILDRED   Yes.

LORETTA   Louis got killed. He's dead?

MILDRED   Yes.

LORETTA   An they're lookin' for Bobby?

MILDRED   They're lookin' for our Bobby.

[*Two sirens begin wailing, growing louder and louder.* MILDRED *and* LORETTA *exit and* BOBBY *sneaks up behind the tent. He violently pulls it down and starts kicking it. He kicks and kicks and kicks. Then he falls exhausted on top of the pile of canvas. He lies rocking as the sirens disappear into the distance*].

SCENE THREE

[NORMAN *is standing over* BOBBY, *looking down at him. They are in the town jail.* NORMAN's *coat has seen better days. Both men are terrified, unable to look at each other. {1967}.*]

BOBBY   We's just friggin' round, just dinkin' round down there. Just talkin', ya know, just tellin' jokes an ... tellin' jokes.

NORMAN   Who all was down there?

BOBBY   There was me and Gordie and Bozo and Bucky.

NORMAN   What about the Hebert kid?

BOBBY   He weren't with us. He just come by. We's just mindin' our own business and he just come by.

NORMAN   Now Bobby, did he say anythin' or do somethin'?

BOBBY   He's laughin' at us.

NORMAN   How come?

110

BOBBY   I donno. 'Cause he thinks he's better. I donno. Says we's all stupid. He's actin' like summer people, ya know. Figure they's better'n we are 'cause they own sailboats off the wharf and we don't.

NORMAN   Bobby, cops say maybe somebody holds that boy down and somebody else kicks'm in the head.

BOBBY   Cops is crazy as the birds.

NORMAN   They say his head smashed up pretty bad. Gonna be closed coffin.

BOBBY   I didn't do it! Didn't do it! Didn't do nothin'!

NORMAN   They say ya did. And ya been in trouble before —

BOBBY   Yeah, but —

NORMAN   For stealin' and breakin' into cottages that time and fightin' —

BOBBY   But —

NORMAN   Raymond Bannister, he says you're best to say you're guilty a manslaughter.

BOBBY   But I didn't do nothin'!

NORMAN   Look now! They found ya all covered with that boy's blood. Cops found your shoes in the ditch out by Ring's Corner. Bannister says one a them's got so much on it, looks like it dyed red. *(Beat)* So he says to plead guilty to manslaughter ya might be okay. He says if they charge ya with second degree, they could send ya up for Life.

BOBBY   Life? But I didn't do nothin'! Swear to God!

[*The men look at each other.*]

NORMAN   Bobby, lookit! Now I donno anythin' 'bout these things, but I trust Bannister.

[NORMAN *gives* BOBBY *a cigarette.*]

NORMAN   His father was Overseas with me.

BOBBY   *(Beat)* Where's Retta?

[*Lights fade on them. A beat, and* NORMAN *leaves.* BOBBY *remains.*]

Scene Four

[JOSSETTE *walks slowly across the beach. It is after the funeral and she is dressed in black {1967}.*]

JOSSETTE   'Member when Lavinia LeBlanc took that big fit and died, and we went to the funeral home to see her? We knew we weren't s'posed to be there, we just went 'cause she's dead and we never seen nobody dead before. We never even knew her really; Louis knew her sister some. And you and Bobby got all freaked out 'cause a her rosary — you thought they got her hands tied up. We shouldn't a been there, we just went 'cause we all double dared each other. *(Beat)* It was springtime, first warm day, and real muddy, so we walked home on the highway. There's still

112

snow in the fields and ice in the bay, but we stopped at the dairy and our brudders bought us ice creams to make us feel better after lookin' at her. They're teenagers that year, and it was weird 'cause they never were friends much. But we's all actin' like we hung out all a time. *(Beat)* When I think 'bout that day, my face gets all hot and I can't get to sleep. I donno how I can see somethin' so bad as Lavinia lyin' there — knowin' how she had a fit waitin' for the bus and fell, knowin' that the funeral guy took all her blood out a her — knowin' all that, I donno how I can remember havin' such a good time walkin' home. And how special we felt when our brudders bought us ice creams. Like we's on a date or somethin'.

[JOSSETTE *walks slowly up the beach and away.*]

SCENE FIVE

[BOBBY is *alone, beside himself with claustrophobia, pacing in a small square of cold light. He talks inaudibly to himself, his voice harsh, a violent whisper. Words occasionally rise to the surface. Both hands are fists and he seems to be talking to them {1967}.*]

BOBBY   *(Mumbles:)* Damn! Dammit! Fuckin' dammit! Jeez dammit jeez! Goddam jeez! I seen I seen I seen! Jeez! Dammit! Whatcha do? Whatcha whatcha? Jeez goddam jeez! Keep your hands off! Keep your jesus hands off! Stupid stupid stupidstupidstupid!

[*He pounds his head with his fists.*

113

Cross fade to next scene. In the half light BOBBY *begins pacing.*]

SCENE SIX

[MILDRED *is sweeping the sand with a broom.* LORETTA *is following close behind her, always at her heels and in her way {1967}.*]

LORETTA   But I don't wanna go to Myrtle and Lawson's.

MILDRED   Retta, we're not gonna argue 'bout it. You always liked your cousin Dottie.

LORETTA   But she's goin' out with that stupid farmer now. She don't want me around. There'll be nothin' to do. Aunt Myrtle won't even let ya play checkers on Sunday, and dancin's a sin. They're a bunch a hicks.

MILDRED   Lawson's comin' down for ya this afternoon and that's that.

LORETTA   But I can't miss Louis's funeral!

MILDRED   You can't go to that. Just get that out a your head. It just isn't right.

LORETTA   But Jossette's my best friend. And Louis was my friend too.

MILDRED   Retta, they're not gonna want you there. Things're changed now. People are gonna be sayin' terrible things. *(Beat)* Look, no more arguments. I don't want ya here for any a this. It's for your own good.

LORETTA   F'I go, s'like sayin' Bobby's guilty.

MILDRED   Oh, don't talk foolish.

LORETTA   But it is. At suppertime that night when I asked'm for his sleepin' bag, he got real mad.

MILDRED   So?

LORETTA   Ya think it's my fault?

MILDRED   What?

LORETTA   That he was fightin' Louis? Cause I made'm mad?

MILDRED   It had nothin' to do with you. That Hebert kid was down there lookin' for a fight.

LORETTA   *(Beat)* You think Bobby done it?

MILDRED   I never said that.

LORETTA   I don't wanna go 'way all by myself.

MILDRED   You're goin' to go. I got enough on my hands without worryin' 'bout you. The whole town's talkin', your poor brother's locked up, your father hasn't been sober for three days —

LORETTA   Dad hasn't been sober for three years.

MILDRED   Don't talk that way 'bout your father! Don'tcha dare talk like that around here!

LORETTA   He's drunk all a time.

MILDRED   Wartime came and buggered everything. He's not the same little fella at all. Somethin' always comes along and buggers everything. Like that damn Hebert kid on the beach the other night.

LORETTA   *(Beat)* Mom, I don't wanna fight. I just wanna stay home.

MILDRED   Retta, you're goin' up country till this mess is straightened out and I don't wanna hear another word about it!

           [MILDRED *exits.*]

LORETTA   Mom? Mom.

           [*She moves to follow her mother then stops, takes a step back. She moves to the crib lies down.* BOBBY *is lying down.*]

           SCENE SEVEN

           [*Lights up slowly on* NORMAN *is alone in the cellar. Drunk. He is looking up, talking through the floor above him. The sound of the speech is very sexual.* BOBBY *and* LORETTA *hear him from their beds {1957}.*]

NORMAN   WOOF! Woofwoofwoofwoofwoof! *(Laughs:)* Don't care. Whaddo I care? *(Sings, loudly, badly:)* "I got my love to keep me warm!" *(Snorts)* Silver sweater big boobs pointed right at me! Right friggin' at me! Bang Bang! *(Laughs:)* Bangbang. *(Hollers:)* SHE WIGGLES HER ARSE AND PURRS LIKE A CAT! *(Beat)* Not like you, that's for damn sure. *(Beat)*

116

WOOF! Woofwoofwoofwoofwoof! Woof.
(Beat) WOOF!

[*He passes out.*]

SCENE EIGHT

[LORETTA *lying in bed.* BOBBY *in jail {1968}.*]

LORETTA

My Louis who art in heaven ... hello. I think I hate my family. I know you're someplace where they say ya got a love your enemies, but I don't think I can love them no mores. Soon as school's over next year, I'm leavin' home, goin' to work. I'll get Uncle Bert to find me a job at the railway, and I won't even take a chair from their house to sit in — not even a cup and saucer. I feel so bad that I never told you how happy I was that time I went over and your mom and dad was in Moncton with Jossette buyin' her shoes, and I stayed and we talked and stuff. 'Bout the teachers at Moncton High and at the French school ya go to and the separatists and that. And ya told me what their songs meant. But I was thinkin' bout how much I wanna walk to the end a the wharf with ya some night in summer. Thinkin' bout you and me movin' away. I wouldn't tell nobody but you that I practised kissin' my own hand later, pretendin' it was you. Stupid, eh? Like Venus Procter when she used to give herself hickies on the arm and say a boy did it. But it weren't like that. *(Beat)* I won't ever love no guy as much as I love you, Louis. I'll divorce my family for you. No guy won't ever be you. Nobody else won't ever be you.

117

[*She covers herself with a sheet.* BOBBY *is lying down.*]

SCENE NINE

[MILDRED *enters, very pregnant. She passes the jail area and covers* BOBBY, *tucks him in very lovingly. She moves to the house area.* Norman *enters, half cut, wearing the coat he wore in scene* [3]. *It is new. He trips over* BOBBY *and enters the kitchen area {1952}.*]

NORMAN   *(Half sings, mumbles:)* "Lili Marlene — "

MILDRED   Normie!

NORMAN   "Lili — "

MILDRED   Norm!

NORMAN   "Marlene"

MILDRED   Little Bobby's asleep!

NORMAN   "I got my love to keep me warm."

MILDRED   Will you be quiet — the kid's finally asleep.

NORMAN   C'mon.

MILDRED   That kid's sick as can be — been throwin' up all day. Took me two and a half hours to get him down.

NORMAN   Gimme a kiss.

MILDRED   I will not.

118

NORMAN   Just a little kiss.

MILDRED   I will not kiss a drunk!

NORMAN   But you're beautiful. *(Sings:)* "Lili Marlene — "

MILDRED   If you've been over at the Legion playin' cards for money again, I'll wring your neck!

NORMAN   "I got my love to keep me warm — "

MILDRED   Stop!

[NORMAN *stops singing. He salutes her, then he lurches towards her, grabs her face and gives her a kiss. She shoves him away. Silence.*]

MILDRED   Keep that dirty filthy thing out of my mouth or so help me God I'll bite right into it!

NORMAN   Millie —

MILDRED   Is it all y'ever think of? Look at me! Just look at me! If you had to go through this I swear to God you'd keep that pecker a yours zipped up tight!

NORMAN   Just a little kiss.

MILDRED   I was not raised to be treated like a slut! I am not one a those French sluts from the wharf!

[*She exits.*]

NORMAN   Who said ya were? Husband's got rights, ya know! A man's got rights! *(Beat)* Ya think you're too good for your own goddam husband? *(Beat)*

What's a man s'posed to do? What the hell's a man to do?

[NORMAN *starts to exit and passes out.*]

SCENE TEN

[LORETTA *wakes up, confused. She hears* MICKEY *talking to his father. She glances over and see* NORMAN*'s body. Lights out on* NORMAN *as soon as* LORETTA *sees him. He leaves in the dark. She gets up and moves to* MICKEY *and* BENOIT.]

MICKEY   Mais papa, pourquoi tu ne viens pas, pourquoi tu ne veins pas toi aussi?

BENOIT   Pas maintenant.

MICKEY   Tu m'as dit que tu me montrerai ou le chevreuil est venu dans to court, et que tu m'ammenerais nager. Papa?

BENOIT   Va avec maman.

[LORETTA *takes* MICKEY *away from* BENOIT. *A look between the parents.* LORETTA *and* MICKEY *are standing outside* MILDRED*'s house. He's wearing a little knapsack {1980}.*]

LORETTA   Now Mickey, don't speak French around Gramma.

MICKEY   Pourquoi pas?

LORETTA   Just cause I said so, okay? She's old fashioned

120

and old fashioned people don't like it
sometimes.

MICKEY   When's Daddy comin'?

LORETTA   Quit askin' me that. We're down here to cheer
           up Gramma and that's that.

MICKEY   But can't Daddy come?

LORETTA   Look, sweetheart, Benny can't, your father can't
           ... Look, not right now ... Just do as your told,
           okay?

MICKEY   How long do we have to stay here?

LORETTA   No more questions, just do as your told. *(Beat)*
           Go find Grammy.

           [*She gives him a little push and walks behind him.
           She stops.* MICKEY *exits. She moves to the jail
           area.*]

           SCENE ELEVEN

           [LORETTA *is beside* BOBBY. *She talks to him
           in prison.* BOBBY *chain smokes, talks like a
           tough, self pitying hood {1970}.*]

LORETTA   It's not very nice in here, is it?

BOBBY   Well it's a friggin' prison, not a summer resort.

LORETTA   *(Beat)* Right. *(Beat)* How's everthin' with you,
           Bobby?

BOBBY   Now what a you think?

121

LORETTA   I donno, I ...

BOBBY   How ya think it is with me stuck in this friggin' lousy Christless hole? *(Beat)* I wish they'd lock that Raymond Bannister up with me.

LORETTA   Oh ...

BOBBY   *(Beat)* Mom says you're lucky to get a job at the CNR.

LORETTA   It's office work, ya know. And it's good to have my own place. Nice little apartment. *(Beat)* I met a guy.

BOBBY   Who?

LORETTA   A guy at work. Ben, Benny. His name's Benoit.

BOBBY   French, eh?

LORETTA   Yeah. His family's from up north. Caraquet.

BOBBY   Bet that made Mom's day.

LORETTA   *(Beat)* You got any friends here or anythin'?

BOBBY   Yeah, I got friends, course I got friends. Good ones. What ya think I am, stupid?

LORETTA   No. I don't, I mean —

BOBBY   I'm in with Ricky Bourque.

LORETTA   The guy who killed the cop? Jesus Bobby, he's a killer!

BOBBY   Ha, what a you knows? He's the most important guy in here.

LORETTA   Oh ... You gonna finish school here or anythin'? Like I hear ya can learn a trade here and stuff like that.

BOBBY   I better get friggin' crackin'. Five years'll fly by and I'll find myself sittin' around outside lookin' for work.

LORETTA   Oh, jeese, Bobby ...

BOBBY   What?

LORETTA   I feel so bad bout everthin'. 'Bout you bein' in here and all.

BOBBY   Yeah. Well, me too, eh?

LORETTA   *(Beat)* I miss stuff we used a do. Like stuff I thought I'd never miss ever. *(Beat)* 'Member when we're kids and Dad took us fishin' up the river in the woods that time? We kept goin' back on our bikes and buildin' a camp up there?

BOBBY   Right.

LORETTA   We went up there once and you found all those dirty magazines hidin' so we knew somebody else knew bout that place. That somebody else was goin' there. Gordie was with us, and his brother ... and somebody else.

BOBBY   Jossette and Louis.

LORETTA   Oh.

BOBBY   I wonder what you's gettin' at.

LORETTA   No.

BOBBY   Then why bring it up, eh?

LORETTA   Just 'cause it's someplace we used a go when
               we were kids, that's all. I liked playin' there,
               that's all.

BOBBY   I think 'bout that place.

LORETTA   Yeah?

BOBBY   'Bout crossin' over the river there where it turns
               and buildin' a little camp right there. Spruce
               grove there. *(Beat)* I was goin' there when the
               cops stop me. Thought I could hide out there a
               couple a days till things blew over. Stupid eh?

LORETTA   What happened?

BOBBY   When?

LORETTA   That night down by the Blue Circle.

BOBBY   You know.

LORETTA   No. I just know what everybody else said 'bout
               it. I know what Mom says and the papers. And
               I hear what Jossette's family says, a little. But
               nobody tells the same story.

BOBBY   What's Jossette say?

LORETTA   We ain't friends no more. *(Beat)* What
               happened?

124

BOBBY	Some people say I got off easy with manslaughter, don't they? They say that.
LORETTA	I donno. They say ya's down at the beach lookin' for a fight.
BOBBY	Me lookin', right. Nobody talks 'bout Louis lookin' though, do they? Hey?
LORETTA	Well, Louis never got in fights.
BOBBY	Right. He's a fuckin' prince. *(Beat)* He said somethin' 'bout you and Jossette.
LORETTA	What?
BOBBY	Somethin' dirty.
LORETTA	Like what?
BOBBY	You don't wanna know.
LORETTA	Tell me.
BOBBY	He said you and Jossette's a couple a queers.
LORETTA	What?
BOBBY	He said you and Jossette's sleepin' out in the tent 'cause you're a couple a queers.
LORETTA	I don't believe you.
BOBBY	You callin' me a liar?
LORETTA	Why would Louis say that?

BOBBY   'Cause he's one himself, that's why.

LORETTA   That's not true.

BOBBY   Right. Ya don't believe me, ya never did. You
               believes your precious Louis. Why's he so
               friggin' special? Who is he, eh? Who? *(Beat)* Get
               out a here.

LORETTA   What?

BOBBY   F'you don't wanna believe your own brother, I
               don't wanna talk to ya no mores.

LORETTA   I just wanna find out what happened.

BOBBY   And when I tell ya, ya don't believe me. Y'ain't
               interested in my truth. Ya cares too much 'bout
               your stupid little frog, y'always did.

LORETTA   No!

BOBBY   Get! Go on, get out! And don't come back! I
               don't wanna see ya here again ever!

               SCENE TWELVE

               [BENOIT *has appeared on the beach.*
               LORETTA *runs to the beach {1970}.*]

LORETTA   Benoit!

               [BENOIT *comes to her.*]

               Look, look out there.

Running Far Back

[*She points at something out in the strait. He looks out at the water.*]

Can you see it? It's a mirage, see? The same lighthouse twice.

BENOIT   Umhum.

[*They look out into the water together. The scene is very sexual.*]

BENOIT   When I was a little kid, about five? Grandmere and I saw the phantom ship of Baie des Chaleurs.

LORETTA   Yeah? What was it like?

BENOIT   I was so little I can't remember much.

LORETTA   Was it big?

BENOIT   Nono, it was far away, and it was at dusk. It had rigging, you know, I could see that. She was very excited.

[*They are sitting together on the sand. The rest of the scene is very physical, with* LORETTA *making the first moves.*]

LORETTA   Do you like Pauline Julien?

BENOIT   What? I guess so, yes. My sister's nuts over her.

LORETTA   I'm crazy over Quebec music.

BENOIT   Yeah?

LORETTA   It's about something, it's really about something. When I was still at home, it drove my mother nuts. "Bring back the Beatles," she said, "Bring back Elvis. Least I didn't hate them this much." She's never happy unless she's complaining.

BENOIT   *(Beat)* What will she say when she sees this?

[*He takes a ring and puts it on her finger.* LORETTA *looks at her engagement ring.*]

LORETTA   She better not say anything.

[*A beat, then she kisses him very aggressively. Then she turns and lies on her stomach, looking at the ring.*]

BENOIT   There is something very important ...

LORETTA   Yes?

BENOIT   *(Touching her back)* You have to let me ...

LORETTA   Yes?

BENOIT   You have to let me kiss you ... on the bum.

LORETTA   *(Laughing:)* On the bum?

BENOIT   Oui — on your big bum.

[*He strokes her bum very gently.*]

LORETTA   You're crazy.

BENOIT   Oui yes you bet.

128

[*He kisses her bum very softly then, when he becomes more aggressive, she stiffens, looks at him. She turns away, then her body softens. The lights fade down on them as they make love throughout the next scene.*]

SCENE THIRTEEN

[MILDRED *and* NORMAN *are visiting* BOBBY *{1971}.*]

MILDRED   She met him at the railway.

BOBBY   What's he like?

MILDRED   He's a damn Frenchman, that's what he's like.

BOBBY   When's it gonna be?

NORMAN   Donno.

MILDRED   "Ecumenical." Know what that means? They'll be married in that damn Assumption Cathedral and they'll let poor old Reverend Lewis in to watch. That's all that means. *(Beat)* Kids'll all be RC.

NORMAN   Now Mother ...

MILDRED   Don't you Now Mother me! Two more years her own brother's stuck in here and does she care? No! No she doesn't! She's too busy galavantin' around the countryside with a damn Frenchman!

BOBBY   She even old enough to get married?

MILDRED   Old enough! She's nineteen! She's no younger than I was. And no smarter either.

[MILDRED *walks away.*]

BOBBY   Married. I can't believe it.

[NORMAN *joins* MILDRED. *Lights fade on* BOBBY.]

NORMAN   That Ben's not so bad, ya know. I think he'll go places.

MILDRED   Of course he'll go places — thanks to Premier Robichaud *they* get every opportunity there is!

NORMAN   Now now ...

MILDRED   You think I don't know why she's marrying him? You think I don't know? She's as bad as my mother — she'd paint her face blue if she thought it would get my goat. My own daughter's turned against me. I haven't had a female to talk to since poor old Lassie was hit by that truck.

[*Lights fade as they exit.*]

SCENE FOURTEEN

[*Darkness. The stage becomes a forest.* BOBBY *escapes from the jail area. There is the sense of danger for* LORETTA *and* BENOIT, *as if* BOBBY *were stalking them. His breathing is heavy {1972}.*]

BOBBY   *(Panting:)* I do — I do — I do — I do — I do — I do — I do — I do —

[*He comes closer to* LORETTA *and* BENOIT. *He stands in front of* LORETTA *and waves a 45 record in front of her {1962}.*]

LORETTA   Gimme that record!

[LORETTA *tries to grab the record.*]

BOBBY   What record?

[LORETTA *jumps away from* BENOIT *and runs after* BOBBY. *Lights down on* BENOIT *who exits. She chases her brother.*]

LORETTA   Gimmee gimmee!

BOBBY   Gimmee Gimmee never gets. It got your name on it?

LORETTA   Yes, yes! Quit it and give it to me Bobby. It's mine!

BOBBY   It got your name on it, huh, your name on it?

LORETTA   YES NOW GIMMEE!

BOBBY   Oh is your name Connie Francis?

LORETTA   Quit it!

BOBBY   Connie! S'Connie Francis! In my house! Can I have your autograph Connie?

LORETTA   Quit it and gimme! I'm goin' to a party and it's number one! Gimmee!

BOBBY   Oh Connie, I'm your biggest fan! Sing for me,

131

will ya? Sing one a your hits. Sing "Lipstick on Your Collar"! "Lipstick on your ca-al-ler, told a tale on you-ou-ou-"

LORETTA   Gimmee my record or I'll-I'll-I'll-

[*She runs after him into the jail/*BOBBY*'s room area.*]

BOBBY   Can I come visit ya in Hollywood, Connie?

LORETTA   BOBBY I'M LATE FOR THE PARTY C'MON!

BOBBY   You're not old enough to go to parties.

[*He holds the record above her head and puts his other arm around her.*]

LORETTA   I'm gonna be in grade five next year and I'm gonna have a boyfriend so give me my record or I'll tell everythin'!

BOBBY   Tell what?

LORETTA   I'll tell everythin'! I'll tell everythin'!

[*A beat, then she grabs the record and runs off. Prison lights back on* BOBBY, *furious at himself.*]

BOBBY   NO NONONONONO!

[*The lights on him begin to fade a few moments into the next scene. {1973} Throughout the next two scenes* BOBBY*'s physical movements become more controlled: by the end of the act he is finally able to stand still.*]

132

SCENE FIFTEEN

[MILDRED *and* LORETTA *are talking.*
NORMAN *is sitting off to one side but*
LORETTA *plays the first part of the scene to her*
father {1973}.]

MILDRED   I knew somethin' like this would happen if he
               left the railway.

LORETTA   Mom, there's nothin' wrong with insurance.

MILDRED   Did insurance build this country? No. It was
               the railway did that. Railway was always good
               enough for this family.

LORETTA   Oh yeah.

               [NORMAN *winks at her.*]

MILDRED   Your grandfather worked in the shops for thirty-
               five years.

LORETTA   Ben's goin' up next week to look for an
               apartment.

NORMAN   Next week.

LORETTA   Yeah.

MILDRED   I thought you and that husband a yours was
               tryin' to have a family.

LORETTA   So?

MILDRED   Movin' up there with that FLQ, you have no
               idea what could happen to ya. Bombin'

133

mailboxes, killin' each other — it's no place to bring up a child.

NORMAN   *(Beat)* Movin' to Montreal, eh?

LORETTA   Yeah. Ben's got a good promotion — he'd be crazy not to take it.

MILDRED   It doesn't matter where ya live, Bobby'll always be your brother.

LORETTA   You think we're leavin' on account a Bobby?

MILDRED   We're not stupid. When his picture was on the front page for escapin' — ya think that was easy for us? But then you had to go and make it worse.

LORETTA   I had to make it worse! It was my wedding!

MILDRED   Couldn't leave well enough alone.

LORETTA   What are you talkin' about?

MILDRED   Tell'r. Go on, tell'r.

NORMAN   Now Mother.

MILDRED   You're as hopeless as she is.

LORETTA   What's the matter now?

MILDRED   Two days after they catch Bobby, who d'ya think your father and me run into at the Dieppe Mall? Dorca, that fat sister a Mavis Hebert's. What in the Name a God did ya think ya were doin'? Have ya lost your mind?

LORETTA   I thought it might make things better. And it was long before Bobby escaped.

MILDRED   Make things better. Askin' those miserable Frenchmen to your weddin'. After the things that were said about us, about Bobby and us, ya had no right to do that. No right at all!

LORETTA   Maybe it was stupid to try and invite Jossette.

MILDRED   Maybe? If she had any brains she'd be dangerous.

LORETTA   I thought there was a chance.

MILDRED   Sure was — a chance to publicly humiliate your poor father and me. D'ja have any idea how the two of us felt when that woman comes marchin' up to us? We was in a store for godsake, and Dorca all holier-than-thou — as usual. Maybe you don't care what people think about you, but at least have some feelin' for your poor father!

LORETTA   I've known Jossette since Grade One.

MILDRED   And if she'd stayed in the French school where she belonged, none a this would a happened. But oh no, they were too good for that.

LORETTA   Ben and I talked about it — we thought the worst she could do was say no.

MILDRED   And did she? Did she? Did she even RSVP, huh?

               [NORMAN *starts to sneak out the door.*]

135

MILDRED   Where do ya think you're goin'?

NORMAN   Eh?

MILDRED   I said where do ya think you're goin'?

NORMAN   I'm goin' out.

MILDRED   Out! And why?

NORMAN   Eh?

MILDRED   Where are ya goin' at this hour?

NORMAN   What?

MILDRED   Where in the Name a God are you goin' at this time a night?

NORMAN   *(Jokingly:)* To see a man about a dog.

           [*He winks at* LORETTA, *exits.*]

MILDRED   WHERE?

NORMAN   *(Off)* TO SEE A FRIGGIN' MAN ABOUT A DOG!

           [*As he exits she shouts after him.*]

MILDRED   Well don't expect me to lug ya up them damn stairs later if ya can't make it to bed under your own steam! *(To Loretta)* Satisfied?

LORETTA   I'll be so glad to see the end a this place.

MILDRED   You've had nothin' to do with this place for years.

136

Go on, take off with your husband, just go.

LORETTA   We just want somethin' we can't get from here.

MILDRED   You donno what ya want, ya never did.

LORETTA   I do so!

MILDRED   Ha.

LORETTA   *(Beat)* And what a you want?

MILDRED   What?

LORETTA   What a you want?

MILDRED   What do I want?

LORETTA   Yeah, tell me. I wanna know.

MILDRED   I want someone to tell me they're sorry. That's all.

LORETTA   Who?

MILDRED   Who? *(Beat)* Everybody! You, your father, the town, the whole damn town. Maisie Buchanan up at the church.

LORETTA   Why?

MILDRED   Why! 'Cause I got it comin'.

LORETTA   Yeah?

MILDRED   Yes! I got it comin' to me for all the crap I had to put up with all a my life in this place! I took second best for as long as I could remember. I

137

was never appreciated at the church or the Ladies Aid or the IODE or when I sold Avon or when I made cherry surprises for all those darn teas or for the time I was in Home and School. Nothin'. I got nothin' for it and I want someone to tell me they are sorry for that. The only person who ever said he was sorry to me was your brother.

LORETTA   Oh.

MILDRED   Yes. Yessiree. On the first day of that damn trial. Your brother said to me, "I'm sorry you got to go through this Mom, I'm real sorry." Only time in my whole life anybody ever apologised to me for anything that really mattered. *(Beat)* Know somethin'? You're gonna find out all too soon that there isn't any more than this. This is it. This is all there is to it.

[MILDRED *exits.* LORETTA *is alone.*]

SCENE SIXTEEN

[JOSSETTE *walks on the beach.* LORETTA *runs to her {1967}.*]

LORETTA   Jossette.

JOSSETTE   Loretta.

LORETTA   I still can't believe it happened. It's the worse thing ever.

JOSSETTE   This mornin' a letter come from the University in Montreal sayin' Louis got accepted.

138

LORETTA	Oh jeese. I wanna go to the funeral but I can't. Mom's makin' me go away today.
JOSSETTE	Doncha dare think about it! If I didn't know ya, none a this would a happen.
LORETTA	You're my best friend.
JOSSETTE	No more. We're movin' away.
LORETTA	Where?
JOSSETTE	I can't tell you.
LORETTA	Jossette, I'm real sorry.
JOSSETTE	Yeah, well, that don't mean nothin'.
LORETTA	I wanna give ya my watch ya always liked.
JOSSETTE	Ya think I'd take it?
LORETTA	I wanna give ya somethin' to keep.
JOSSETTE	Bobby give that to ya. S'got killer fingerprints all over it.
LORETTA	Aw, please, Jossette. Ya knows I love Louis!
JOSSETTE	Don't even say his name!
LORETTA	But it's true!
JOSSETTE	Who cares, it don't count. Doncha dare cry for him, ya got no right! I'm not even s'posed to talk to ya, ever again.

LORETTA   *(Beat)* This is it then? We won't ever be friends again?

JOSSETTE   It ain't allowed. I'm goin'.

             [*She starts to go.*]

LORETTA   Bobby's a hood! I promise I hate'm!

JOSSETTE   Nothin' ya say'll make it better. *(Beat)* Know what my Dad says? You're nothin', you're never gonna amount to nothin'. Just like your brother!

             [*She leaves.*]

LORETTA   That's a lie! I ain't! I ain't nothin'! I ain't nothin'! I'm as good as you! I am!

             [LORETTA *gets down on her knees. She takes off her watch and buries it in the sand. The gentle sound of waves fades in.* LORETTA *goes to* BENOIT *in Montreal area. She stands behind him, watching him and then suddenly touches him. He turns to her {1974}.*]

LORETTA   Benny!

BENOIT   What?

LORETTA   Guess.

BENOIT   What?

LORETTA   I'm pregnant.

BENOIT   *(Thrilled:)* Yeah?

LORETTA   Yeah, finally. Doctor says it's for sure.

BENOIT   *(A beat, then he laughs:)* Holy shit, a baby!

             [*She lets him kiss her. In his area,* BOBBY *is standing very still.*]

BENOIT   Everything is perfect.

             [JOSSETTE *walks past* LORETTA.]

JOSSETTE   You're nothin'!

BENOIT   Everything is perfect.

LORETTA   S'gonna be a beautiful baby.

             [JOSSETTE *walks past the jail area and spits the line at* BOBBY.]

JOSSETTE   Te rien!

             [JOSSETTE *exits.* LORETTA *is sitting with her arms wrapped around her legs, knees tucked under her chin.* BENOIT *sits beside her.* BOBBY *watches* LORETTA, *slowly taking off his shirt.* BENOIT *touches her, she looks at him and then away, hugging her legs tighter. As* BOBBY *speaks,* BENOIT *gets on his knees behind* LORETTA. *He kisses her neck, touches her very gently.* BOBBY *slowly leaves the jail area, looking at* LORETTA. *By the end of* BOBBY's *speech,* LORETTA *is lying back in her husband's lap.*]

BOBBY   When Mom and Dad's downstairs talkin' in the

kitchen — talkin' in that way I know they'll say, "Go and watch TV" if I go in there — I go up to your room 'bout an hour after your bedtime, I go up when ya's sleepin'. You're so soft. Your mouth's open in a little circle and I touch your lips real soft with my finger, movin' it round the circle, not wantin' to wake ya up. Or maybe I kiss your cheek, softer'n anythin' — pillows, foam rubber, anythin'. And I think you're the most special thing that ever happened. And I can't get over it — your hair, everythin'. I can still see your little legs all round in that pink dress ya wore to Sunday School. I can't say it right, can't say how I feel, but it's more better, more better'n anythin'.

LORETTA   S'gonna be a beautiful baby.

[*Lights fade to black.*]

END OF ACT ONE

ACT TWO

SCENE ONE

[*Dark and the sound of wind. Half light on Montreal areas:* BENOIT *is sleeping and* LORETTA *is sitting on the side of the bed. In his area,* MICKEY *is sitting up in bed, asleep. Lights up on beach.* NORMAN *is walking, drunk. Lights out on Montreal area.*]

NORMAN   (*Sings, mumbles:*) When He cometh, when He cometh
To make up His jewels,
All his jewels, precious jewels,
His loved and His own,

Like the stars of the morning,
His bright crown adorning,
They shall shine in their beauty
Bright gems for His crown.

[*Lights fade on him as he exits and up on* MILDRED *and* BOBBY *in jail {1974}.* LORETTA *and* BENOIT *are in bed {1979}.*]

MILDRED   He's born less'n two hours after we get Retta to that hospital. Easiest delivery this family ever had, I swear: little fella just jumps out a her rarin' to go — and they's both back home next day. No reason for me to stay up in Montreal at all. Retta didn't need me one little bit.

BOBBY   Is he cute?

143

MILDRED His father won't admit it, but little Mickey don't look like him at all. *(Smiles:)* He looks just like us. He's got your face Bobby. He's got your little face.

[BENOIT *touches* LORETTA's *leg she moves away slightly*].

LORETTA Ben.

BOBBY Wish I could see'm.

[MILDRED *exits. Lights down on jail area.* BOBBY *exercises.* BENOIT *walks his fingers along* LORETTA's *side. She turns her back to him and he caresses her.*]

BENOIT Loretta?

LORETTA What?

BENOIT I'm just a poor pilgrim at the shrine of your bum.

LORETTA Oh, jeese, no stupid sex jokes tonight, okay?

BENOIT When my mother and father were our age, they had five kids.

LORETTA Look, we've already talked about it.

BENOIT No, we haven't. Each time I try to, you hit the roof.

LORETTA There's nothing to say.

BENOIT I think we should have another baby. Mickey

144

should have a little brother, little sister. It's not right to have just one.

LORETTA   Ben, Mickey is all I can handle, and that's that. One kid's hard enough. Two just makes it worse.

BENOIT   Not every family is like yours you know.

LORETTA   *(Beat)* Touché.

BENOIT   *(Beat)* The Buctouche Beehive is back at work.

LORETTA   Yeah? How was her holiday down home?

BENOIT   No jellyfish. She brought back some dulce.

LORETTA   Don't offer me any.

[*They sit a moment. He looks at her, she ignores him.*]

LORETTA   Pas de jellyfish, eh?

BENOIT   I want to move back to New Brunswick, that's all. I miss it, okay?

LORETTA   Why?

BENOIT   Why? The land around grandmere's house is getting all built up — I want Mickey to see it before it's all gone.

LORETTA   Aw, gee.

BENOIT   What the hell's wrong with you?

LORETTA   Nothing. *(Beat)* Why can't you just hate it! Bunch a stupid hicks sitting around moaning about how poor they are. Nobody does anything, they just sit around on their asses moaning about how they started the goddam country and how the goddam country abandoned them. My mother's still bitching about when the Shops burnt and they rebuilt them twenty miles away!

BENOIT   So?

LORETTA   So? So the fire was a hundred years ago! It's no goddam wonder half of them are on welfare — they don't know the meaning of the word "future!" I don't want that kid in there to be a part of any of that!

[*Behind them* MICKEY *enters in pyjamas. He walks past them.*]

LORETTA   Mickey? Shit, we woke him up. Mickey?

[*He keeps walking.*]

BENOIT   Mickey? He's asleep.

LORETTA   He's walking in his sleep!

BENOIT   Mickey? Should we wake him up?

LORETTA   I don't think you're supposed to.

BENOIT   I don't want him to fall.

[BENOIT *walks behind* MICKEY.]

146

LORETTA   Do you suppose he's dreaming?

BENOIT   What if he starts to go outside?

LORETTA   Bring him back to bed.

                 [BENOIT *suddenly giggles.* LORETTA *laughs too.*]

LORETTA   Bring him now.

                 [BENOIT *picks* MICKEY *up, carries him back to bed. They lie down with* MICKEY *between them.*]

LORETTA   Poor little guy.

BENOIT   It doesn't mean a bad dream, does it?

                 [MICKEY'*s legs begin to twitch very fast.* LORETTA *and* BENOIT'*s voices have softened. He touches* MICKEY *and his wife.*]

BENOIT   Look. He's dreaming that he's running.

LORETTA   He's like a dog. Bobby and I used to watch Lassie do this when we were kids.

MICKEY   Oh.

BENOIT   He's waking up.

LORETTA   What is it, dear? You have a bad dream?

MICKEY   What?

LORETTA   You were dreaming.

147

MICKEY   Is it my birthday?

LORETTA   No.

MICKEY   Oh.

BENOIT   Mickey? *(Beat)* He's sleeping again.

               [BENOIT*'s hand pushes* LORETTA*'s hair back
               from her face. He looks at her.*]

BENOIT   He's handsome, eh? Et tu est tellement belle, je
               voudrais te manger. *(Beat)* I'll take him back to
               his bed.

LORETTA   No!

BENOIT   What?

LORETTA   No. Let him stay right here.

               [*She snuggles close to* MICKEY.]

BENOIT   He's fine now, give him back.

LORETTA   No. He'll stay right here with his Mommy.

               [*Crossfade.*]

               SCENE TWO

               [NORMAN *visits* BOBBY *in Dorchester
               {1978}.*]

NORMAN   Your mother tells me that you're boxin'.

BOBBY   Right.

148

NORMAN   Good money in that — lookit Yvon Durrell.

BOBBY   You ever box any?

NORMAN   Me? You kiddin'? No sir. I'll leave the fightin' to you. I'm no good at that.

BOBBY   *(Beat)* F'I didn't take off that time, I'd be out a here now.

NORMAN   Not much longer.

BOBBY   What a you know? You ain't never been locked up.

NORMAN   No sir. No I ain't. 'Cept for that time your mother locked me in the cellar. She's madder'n a wet hen that time, eh? *(Beat)* But, no sir, I ain't never been locked up. I been Overseas.

BOBBY   Right.

NORMAN   Know what I come back with?

BOBBY   What?

NORMAN   *(Laughs:)* Nothin'.

BOBBY   You got a medal, right?

NORMAN   What?

BOBBY   You got a ribbon in the War.

NORMAN   Where?

BOBBY   Used a keep it in your top drawer.

NORMAN   What was you doin' in my top drawer?

BOBBY   Lookin' for nickels for the movies. Takin' Retta
          to the movies. That's when we saw it first. It's a
          ribbon, right?

NORMAN   A ribbon.

BOBBY   Yeah. Retta used a tie up her doll's hair in it.

NORMAN   She took it out a that drawer?

BOBBY   She always put it back.

NORMAN   Can't keep a damn thing to yourself, can't have
          any privacy whatsoever. She had no business
          playin' with that.

BOBBY   We didn't hurt nothin'.

NORMAN   That top drawers no place for kids.

BOBBY   She just liked it 'cause it's pretty.

NORMAN   It's the only goddam thing I got to show for
          that whole goddam war — you kids had no
          right playin' with it! She had no right puttin'
          my Nazi Iron Cross Ribbon on a doll!

BOBBY   That's a Nazi ribbon?

NORMAN   You betcha.

BOBBY   How'd ya get it?

NORMAN   I took it off a German in Holland.

BOBBY   Yeah?

NORMAN   Frenchman from Pre D'en Haut got one, so we all wanted one too, all the guys in my outfit. Bunch a stupid kids, most a us. You kids had no right playin' with it!

BOBBY   What happen to this German guy?

NORMAN   I's comin' round this corner when I sees this fella. Almost bump into him sittin' there. And first I's surprised cause he's a dead ringer for A.C. Bridges.

BOBBY   Who?

NORMAN   Marvin Bridges son. A.C. used a live over by the wharf. Oh before your time, long before. But me bein' slow on the uptake there, I'm thinkin' "Now what's A.C. doin' dressed like a German?" Then I remember, old A.C.'s dead, drowned in a squall fishin' lobsters off P.E.I. and I saw that ribbon.

BOBBY   Yeah?

NORMAN   We's closer'n you and me when I shot'm. Then I ripped the ribbon off a his shirt and took off.

BOBBY   How come ya didn't get a Canadian ribbon for it?

NORMAN   What?

BOBBY   For bravery or somethin'?

NORMAN   Bravery? Half the medals they dole out for bein'

brave they should give ya just for bein' stupid
enough to be there in the first place.

BOBBY   Why's that?

NORMAN   Just a kid, younger lookin'n me then. And him
               with an Iron Cross.

BOBBY   He go for his gun?

NORMAN   He's dead 'fore he ever knew what hit'm. *(Beat)*
               Ya know, mostimes ya donno what you're doin'
               till it's too late, and by then, you're sunk. *(Beat)*
               We's in the doghouse, Bobby Boy. You and me.
               We's in the doghouse.

               [BOBBY *and* NORMAN *look each other in the
               eye, very briefly, then* NORMAN *lower his head.*
               BOBBY *watches him as they sit quietly.*
               Crossfade. NORMAN *and* BOBBY *leave the
               stage.*]

               SCENE THREE

               [BENOIT *is kneeling in front of* MICKEY,
               brushing his hair. MICKEY *fidgets a bit but
               stands still.* BENOIT *pushes the hair away from*
               MICKEY'*s forehead very gently.* LORETTA *is to
               one side watching them, staring at* BENOIT'*s
               hands.*]

LORETTA   What happened to your hands? They're all
               changed. They're all sweaty now. Little
               hangnails on your fingers and your nails look
               all smashed up and stupid — like they're too
               small. Little runty nails — don't even have any
               moons. *(Beat)* Louis had the nicest hands —

not like yours, or Bobby's always stuck in some old car. Dad said, "Don't marry a man with nice hands, means he's never worked a day in his life." As if he knew anything. When we brought Mickey home from the hospital, Mom says, "Look at those little fingers, just like little baby shrimps. Bobby's were just like them." All the time she's stayin' with us, all I can think of is that if she doesn't get on that train and get the hell out a here, I'm gonna slam somebody's fingers in a car door.

[*She stands very still.*]

BENOIT　　　There, bon.

[BENOIT *pokes* MICKEY *in the stomach with his finger.* MICKEY *laughs, grabs his fathers finger.*]

MICKEY　　　Estomac! Estomac!

[BENOIT *drops his shoulders, feigns exhaustion.*]

BENOIT　　　Non.

MICKEY　　　Oui.

BENOIT　　　Non non.

MICKEY　　　Oui oui.

BENOIT　　　Non non non.

MICKEY　　　Oui oui oui.

[MICKEY *pretends to hit his father with his fists.*]

153

BENOIT   Okay. Estomac.

[MICKEY *stands still with his arms out from his sides. He tries not to laugh as his father tickles him in a different place with each word.*]

BENOIT   Estomac de plomb *(Stomach)* — Gorge de pigeon *(Chest)* — Menton fourchu *(Chin)* — Goule d'argent *(Mouth)* — Joue bouillie *(Cheek)* — Joue routie *(Other cheek)* — Nez quinquin *(Nose)* — P'tit oeil *(Eye)* — Gros-t-oeil *(Other eye)* — Poque la mailloche!

[BENOIT *starts to tap* MICKEY *on the forehead but he quickly moves his hands down and tickles him under the arms.* MICKEY *screams with laughter and runs to* LORETTA.]

MICKEY   Mommy Mommy Mommy Mommy!

[*He grabs* LORETTA'*s leg.* BENOIT *is close behind him. He grabs* MICKEY, *laughing.* LORETTA *recoils.* MICKEY *runs off laughing, a beat and* BENOIT *follows. Then* LORETTA *moves to follow but stays on stage. Crossfade.*]

Scene Four

[BOBBY *is standing alone. Ocean sounds. He is wearing a cheap suit. The space around him seems huge. A sense of great distance. The light grows brighter, as if the sun were coming up behind him. He is nervous {1979}.*
Both BOBBY *and* LORETTA *are on stage; in a moment she will exit.*
MILDRED *arrives with a chair for him. Up*

154

until NORMAN*'s arrival she is almost hyper: girlish and flirtatious.*]

MILDRED   Here's a chair for ya, dear. Just have a seat, don't try to do too much all at once.

[*He sits down slowly.*]

MILDRED   There. *(Beat)* Place's changed a little, hasn't it? I tried to keep ya up on most of it, but there's a few surprises. Ya like the new kitchen?

BOBBY   Yeah.

[MILDRED *leaves.* LORETTA *exits the stage from her area.* BOBBY *is very awkward.* MILDRED *comes back with a table/tray which she places in front of him. On the tray is a piece of cake and a small parcel, wrapped with a bow on it.*]

MILDRED   I made it last night. It's my pineapple upside down cake you like so much. And I got your favourite juice. And this is for you.

BOBBY   Mom, you didn't have —

MILDRED   It's just a little something from your stupid old mother.

[*He holds the gift, examines it.*]

BOBBY   Where's Dad?

MILDRED   Down at Romeo's more'n likely. He'll be home soon enough. Go ahead.

[*He slowly opens the gift.*]

MILDRED   I baked that clam casserole ya always liked. Won't take twenty minutes to heat it up for lunch.

[BOBBY *is looking at a white shirt and tie.*]

MILDRED   I've got the slip if it doesn't suit your fancy.

[*He looks at her, half a shrug, half a smile.*]

MILDRED   And there's an envelope in there too. The man at Colpitts has a suit for ya. We'll just go in and pick out the one ya want. You won't have to wear that old suit from Dorchester.

BOBBY   Thanks Mom.

MILDRED   It's not much.

[NORMAN *is standing off to one side.*]

NORMAN   Bobby.

BOBBY   Hi Dad.

[*The men shake hands, almost embarrassed by the gesture.*]

NORMAN   Well, when'd you get in?

BOBBY   Mom and I just got back.

NORMAN   She was out a the house like a shot at the crack a dawn.

MILDRED   I was not! It was after nine and you were dead to the world.

NORMAN   Well sir. Well sir. Welcome back.

MILDRED   You been over to Romeo's today?

NORMAN   No.

MILDRED   You goin'?

NORMAN   Eventually. Whatcha got there, Bobby?

BOBBY   Shirt and tie.

NORMAN   Oh, I see. I see.

[BOBBY *holds out the shirt to him. Just as* NORMAN *takes it:*]

MILDRED   Wash your hands before ya touch it.

NORMAN   My hands are clean. Sides, it's all wrapped up in cellophane.

MILDRED   I had a little talk with Al LeBlanc at the Garage. He says his son's movin' out west and he might be able to use a hand. Said maybe ya'd drop in on'm in the next couple a days. No hurry, he says.

NORMAN   Get your sea legs first.

[*A long pause.*]

You should come take a look at what they're buildin' down there at that wharf next to Romeo's.

157

BOBBY   Yeah?

NORMAN   Just gonna be another make-work project, not
            worth a tinker's damn.

MILDRED   He doesn't need to see that mess.

NORMAN   *(Laughs:)* Kind a hard to miss, ain't it?

MILDRED   He doesn't need to traipse off to see the likes a
            that first thing.

NORMAN   I bet he's dyin' to walk down there, smell that
            good salt air, see the old boys. Aren't ya Bobby
            boy?

MILDRED   We just got in the house this minute!

NORMAN   Now Mother, whoa down there.

MILDRED   Don't you "Now Mother" me.

NORMAN   Calm yourself.

BOBBY   *(Beat)* I think ...

MILDRED   Yes dear?

BOBBY   I think maybe I'll go for a walk.

MILDRED   Have some cake before ya go.

BOBBY   I'm not really hungry Mom. I'll have it later.

MILDRED   Ya haven't eaten a thing all day.

NORMAN   Don't hound the boy.

MILDRED   I'm not houndin'm! He doesn't have to go down to see that mess at Romeo's right now.

NORMAN   I never said he did!

MILDRED   We just got in the house this instant!

[NORMAN *winks at* BOBBY.]

MILDRED   Quit winkin' at'm like I'm some god damn fool! I am not houndin' a damn soul!

[BOBBY *nervously stands up. He knocks the little table over and the cake falls on the ground.*]

BOBBY   Oh.

MILDRED   Oh no. Look, just look at that.

[*No one moves.*]

NORMAN   That your upside down cake?

MILDRED   *(Beat)* Dammit! Dammitall to hell!

[MILDRED *leaves.*]

NORMAN   Don't pay any attention to her.

BOBBY   Dad —

NORMAN   Let's go find old Romeo. He's got some a that good Jamaican rum. Five thousand proof! *(Laughs)*

BOBBY   I'm not ...

NORMAN   You're not what? Ya won't even have a drink with your old man? Whatcha gonna do, have tea with her?

          [BOBBY *stands very still, looks at his father.*]

BOBBY   No, I'm goin' for a walk by myself, down along the shore.

NORMAN   She'll have ya all aproned up bakin' squares.

BOBBY   Look Dad, don't say a word against her, you've got no right to say a word against her.

NORMAN   Just a joke.

BOBBY   No, s'not a joke. If ya'd paid attention to her once in a while the two a ya wouldn't always be at each other like a couple a dogs.

NORMAN   Oh take her side, take her side, everybody always does.

BOBBY   I'm not takin' sides, I'm just tellin' ya that long as I'm here, I don't wanna hear ya makin' fun a her to me. I got no time for ya.

NORMAN   *(Beat)* Well. *(Beat)* Wellsir.

          [NORMAN *looks at* BOBBY, *then away. He shakes his head.*]

NORMAN   Frig.

          [NORMAN *leaves.* BOBBY *looks down at the cake.*]

160

BOBBY   HEY! You! Who do you think you are, eh? Who
               do you ...

               [*He starts to kick at the cake, then he stops. He
               sinks to his knees and picks it up, puts it on the
               plate. He starts to cry. He is sobbing as sits back in
               the chair and picks and brushes the sand from the
               cake. Lights fade.*]

               SCENE FIVE

               [LORETTA *rages in wearing a wedding dress.*
               BENOIT *follows her in a suit {1972}.*]

LORETTA   Driving through a goddam roadblock set up for
               my goddam brother on the way to my own
               goddam wedding! Jesus christ! *(Beat)* I can't go
               back in there!

BENOIT   It will be worse if you hide out in here. The
               goddam little shit.

LORETTA   Oh god, it's so tacky, just so goddam tacky. Your
               mother must hate me.

BENOIT   Nobody thinks this has anything to do with
               you.

LORETTA   No?

BENOIT   No.

LORETTA   That cop said he robbed a garage. Robbed a
               garage and took off into the woods.

               [BENOIT *tries to comfort her, she moves away in
               a rage.*]

LORETTA   He's buggered my life from the start! Why today? Why the hell would he pick today?

BENOIT   It's got nothing to do with you.

LORETTA   You think so! Ha. Off hidin' in the woods like some stupid kid! Like a stupid kid! I'm ashamed to show my face at my own goddam wedding! Dad's out there ready to fall over — Mom's chompin' at the bit to get home and listen to police reports on the radio. Some goddam wedding this is! Thank the living God Jossette didn't show up!

BENOIT   They'll catch him soon. It'll be all over soon.

LORETTA   Oh God, they're chasin' after him with guns and dogs!

          [*She starts to cry.* BENOIT *goes to her. She lets him hold her.*]

BENOIT   S'okay, s'okay. We'll just go out there for half an hour, okay? Twenty minutes. Then we'll go to a hotel. We won't leave for P.E.I. till tomorrow — by then the whole thing will be over.

LORETTA   You think so?

BENOIT   Yes.

LORETTA   But the wedding's ruined.

BENOIT   No. We're married, aren't we?

LORETTA   But I wanted it to be perfect!

BENOIT   It will be. *(Kisses her)* We've got a house on Jones Lake. *(Kisses her again)* We're gonna have babies. Right?

LORETTA   Big fat bilingual babies.

BENOIT   *(Laughs)* Oui. You bet. So it will be perfect. We'll be like my Aunt Marie and Uncle Ferdinand. In twenty-five years, the kids, they'll all get together and send us to Disneyland.

LORETTA   You really think they'll catch him today?

BENOIT   Where can he go?

LORETTA   *(Beat)* Goddam guns and dogs. The poor stupid arsehole.

BENOIT   Come on. We'll wash your face and go back for a minute. *(Beat)* Come on.

LORETTA   Benoit?

BENOIT   Oui?

LORETTA   Je t'aime.

            [*He kisses her again, takes her hand and leads her off.*]

BENOIT   Et t'es tellement belle, je voudrais te manger. *(He repeats it, making her laugh)* Et t'es tellement belle, je voudrais te manger. Et t'es tellement belle, je voudrais te manger.

            [*Both* BOBBY *and* LORETTA *have left the stage.*]

163

SCENE SIX

[NORMAN *is on the beach at night. He is walking home, drunk. Maybe he sings to himself, but it is under his breath, barely audible. He giggles quietly. Everything amuses him. He stops and looks about him, sees no one, then opens his fly and takes out his pecker. He breathes a sigh of relief then giggles for a second as he begins to write his name in the sand with a steady stream of pee. He writes two letters, laughs, then his body goes stiff and his hands fly out from his sides. He is dead before he hits the sand {1980}. Fade to black.*]

SCENE SEVEN

[LORETTA *and* BENOIT *in Montreal. She is packing, folding a blouse and putting it in an overnight bag.* MICKEY *is asleep {1980}. In kitchen area,* BOBBY *is sitting in the chair. {1980}*]

BENOIT   Are you sure you don't want me to come?

LORETTA   Yeah yes. Yes I'm sure.

BENOIT   Because I think I should.

LORETTA   No, it's easier this way.

BENOIT   Oh. How long are you going to be there? With your family?

LORETTA   I can't say, I don't know. You know, after the funeral and seeing how Mom is and ...

164

BENOIT   I think I should go.

LORETTA   No Benny, let's ...

BENOIT   I'm going to have to find someone to look after Mickey anyway and —

LORETTA   I'm taking Mickey.

BENOIT   What?

LORETTA   You're always talking about how you want him to see New Brunswick. I'm taking Mickey and going home.

BENOIT   I wasn't taking about taking him down there for a funeral. Your brother's at home.

LORETTA   I know.

BENOIT   I don't want my son to have anything to do with him.

LORETTA   "My son, *my* son!" God, I hate it when men say that! Mickey is *our* son and if I want to take him —

BENOIT   I don't want him to have anything to do with your brother.

LORETTA   Neither do I!

BENOIT   I'm coming.

LORETTA   No.

BENOIT   Then leave Mickey here.

LORETTA   I'm taking Mickey and going home.

BENOIT   Why?

LORETTA   *(Beat)* Because I'm leaving you.

BENOIT   What?

LORETTA   I'm leaving you, I don't love you.

BENOIT   *(Beat)* What?

LORETTA   Oh please don't make me say it again.

BENOIT   Calice, don't make you say it again. But sure, we should make it easy on you. We should let you off the hook, eh?

LORETTA   Oh God.

BENOIT   You just announce it and that's fine, that's it. "Good-bye I'm taking your son and getting the hell out of here." Perfect. Everything makes sense now, every damn thing starts to make sense.

LORETTA   I'm sorry.

BENOIT   Oh, then it's all right, she is sorry. My wife is sorry. What the hell is going on?

LORETTA   I've tried and tried but I don't, I don't feel it!

BENOIT   Have I been bad to you? That it? Hit you? Lock you away? Say "No you can't do that?"

LORETTA   No. Nonononono.

166

BENOIT   What then? Where the fuck am I wrong?

LORETTA   I just don't love you. That's all.

BENOIT   That's all.

LORETTA   I can't help it!

BENOIT   You can try!

LORETTA   I have I have I have I have!

[MICKEY *was woken up.*]

MICKEY   Mommy?

LORETTA   *(Furiously:)* Get back to your bed! Get out a here and get back to bed right now!

BENOIT   Don't talk to him like that!

LORETTA   Don't you tell me how to talk to him! Doncha dare!

BENOIT   Don't shout at him! Don't use that voice with him!

LORETTA   Don't tell me what to do!

BENOIT   Don't tell you?! You the big boss here now?! You make all the decisions?! Jesus Christ, you say do this, you say do that! You dragged me to this fucking city! You think you can throw me out of both your lives and I just stand here! You bitch!

[*She throws the blouse at him.*]

167

LORETTA   Don't call me that you stupid fro —

               [*She hides her head in her hands.* BENOIT *is
               trying not to cry.* MICKEY *runs out behind his
               parents' backs.*]

BENOIT   For ten years I hear you bitch about your
               mother, and now I find I'm married to her all
               along.

               [*A long moment as they look at each other. Then
               she turns to where* MICKEY *was standing.*]

LORETTA   MICKEY!

               [*She runs out after him. A beat, then* BENOIT
               lifts the blouse to his face. Fade.]

               SCENE EIGHT

               [LORETTA *runs after* MICKEY *but can't find
               him. She finds herself in the kitchen looking at*
               BOBBY. *Long beat as they look at each other
               {1980}.*
               MILDRED*'s voice is heard in the background —
               she gradually comes into the scene. Everything is
               tense.* MILDRED *is trying to ease tensions by
               talking.*]

MILDRED   I've got to call Maisie Buchanan with a hymn
               for the service. Are their any objections to
               "When He Cometh"? I know it's a Sunday
               School hymn, but your father liked it. He used
               to sing it to you kids when you were little. And
               it's not mournful, I hate those mournful things.

BOBBY   "When He Cometh" is fine Mom.

MILDRED   Your father used to sing it with you kids.

[MILDRED *is standing with her children.*]

MILDRED   I wish it was all over. I hate a fuss. I just hate people makin' a fuss. Maisie brought over some date squares. What are we gonna do with all those squares? Everybody and his dog brought some. What'll we ever do with them all?

BOBBY   We can stick'm in the freezer.

MILDRED   But they'll all want their pans back. *(Beat)* I'll take'm over to the boat people.

LORETTA   What?

MILDRED   The squares.

BOBBY   Mom, not tonight.

MILDRED   We'll never eat them all. *(Beat)* I'm on their food committee. *(Beat)* You know something? I don't think they'll stay here. They'll be happier where there's more of their own kind. And wouldn't ya know, the women at the RC Church are taking them out to the French Bingo.

LORETTA   So?

MILDRED   So it's only about one thing.

LORETTA   What?

MILDRED   They don't want them speaking English.

LORETTA   Oh for godsakes.

MILDRED   It's true.

LORETTA   It is not.

MILDRED   There is nothing wrong with English Bingo!

            [*Beat, then* MICKEY *comes in.*]

MILDRED   There's the little angel.

LORETTA   You've got mud all over your good pants.

MILDRED   Just a little dirt, nothin' we can't brush out, is it,
            Mickey?

LORETTA   Take your pants off and I'll go hang them up.

MICKEY   I wanna go back outside.

LORETTA   No it's gettin' late.

MILDRED   Let the boy go outside.

LORETTA   Mom, it's almost dark, he's had a long day.

MICKEY   They're playin' hide'n-go-seek.

BOBBY   They'll be there tomorrow.

MILDRED   Oh, come on Mom, don't be such an old
            meanie.

LORETTA   Mom.

MILDRED   That little Petipas girl's been waitin' for him all
            day. She was over here this morning when her
            mother brought those squares.

170

LORETTA   Mickey, go get those pants off.

MICKEY   Nope.

[*She moves towards* MICKEY, *but he grins and goes behind* BOBBY.]

MILDRED   He's determined. It's too bad Ben couldn't come down for the funeral.

LORETTA   Yeah. Mickey, march.

MILDRED   Just a little bit longer, Mom.

LORETTA   Mom, for chrissake.

BOBBY   *(Beat)* Mickey?

MICKEY   Yeah, Uncle Bobby?

BOBBY   C'mere. Lemme see your pants.

[BOBBY *has taken a big clean handkerchief out of his pocket and starts to brush the dust off* MICKEY's *pants with it.*]

MICKEY   Jocelyn says her mother let's her stay up till ten and later in the summer. They go swimming sometimes after dark and take all their clothes off. And sometimes they all sleep at the beach and have marshmallows.

LORETTA   Mickey, come here. Don't bother your uncle.

BOBBY   He's no bother, are ya dear? Nothin' here a little lick won't get rid of.

[BOBBY *licks the handkerchief and uses it to rub at a spot on* MICKEY*'s pants.*]

BOBBY   Tickle Man's comin'.

MILDRED   He sure loves his uncle, don'tcha dear?

BOBBY   Coochy coochy coochy.

             [BOBBY *tickles* MICKEY *and he laughs.*]

LORETTA   Mickey, what did I say to you?

BOBBY   You want me to show ya how to box?

             [LORETTA *violently grabs* MICKEY *and pulls him away from* BOBBY. *He runs back to his uncle.* LORETTA *grabs him again, pushes him roughly.*]

LORETTA   Do as you're told!

             [MICKEY *runs away from her and out onto the beach.*]

MILDRED   There was no need for you to do that! No damn need of that at all!

LORETTA   Quit pushin' me!

MILDRED   Who's doin' the pushin'?

LORETTA   You! You've been pushin' me all my life! And takin' everythin' away from me from the day I was born!

MILDRED   You're still mopin' cause ya missed Expo 67.

172

LORETTA   Expo 67 has nothing to do with Louis Hebert!

[LORETTA *runs out after* MICKEY.]

LORETTA   Mickey! Mickey!

MILDRED   Everything's buggered.

[*She looks at* BOBBY *and then moves away. She leaves.* BOBBY *alone. Fade.*]

SCENE NINE

[*Darkness. A storm.* MICKEY *runs across the beach and stands looking very frightened. In the darkness around him,* MILDRED *and* NORMAN *move across the sand. They are heard and felt rather than seen: a fury raging in the dark.* LORETTA *enters looking for her son. He comes to her. She holds him, sits down and holds him in her lap {1980/1956}.*]

LORETTA   Mickey!

NORMAN   Millie!

MILDRED   Don't even come near me!

NORMAN   Just listen to me!

MILDRED   I can't even feed those kids in there!

NORMAN   Just listen!

[*During this,* BOBBY *appears beside* LORETTA. BOBBY *and* LORETTA *are young children.*]

MILDRED   I can't even feed those kids a decent meal and
               you lost every goddam cent to that tribe down
               at the Legion!

NORMAN   But —

MILDRED   Ya fell down, all covered in mud —

NORMAN   *(Pathetic, almost crying:)* Just one more try, let's
               give it one more try!

BOBBY   *(Whispers:)* Don't be afraid.

LORETTA   *(Whispers:)* I ain't.

MILDRED   If you start to cry, you'll be out that door in the
               mud so fast —

NORMAN   Millie —

               [BOBBY *is touching* LORETTA.]

MILDRED   I can smell her! How stupid do ya think I am?
               I can smell that trash before you opened the
               door!

LORETTA   You gonna stay with me?

BOBBY   You want me to?

LORETTA   Mom'll get mad if she finds ya in my bed.

NORMAN   *(Crying:)* No, no —

MILDRED   Ya stink to high heaven! Get out a this house
               until you're sober!

LORETTA   She spanked me just cause I hate liver.

BOBBY   I snuck mine to the dog when she wasn't lookin'.

LORETTA   Take me swimmin' tomorrow, buy me some chips?

            [*He has his arm around her. She starts to giggle.*]

BOBBY   Ssssh.

LORETTA   Tickles.

BOBBY   That better?

LORETTA   Why's Dad cryin'?

BOBBY   He's just drunk. Coochy coochy.

            [LORETTA *lets out a loud whoop of laughter.*]

MILDRED   You kids shuttup and quit foolin' around or so help me God I'm comin' up there with a hairbrush to tan your hides!

            [*A beat. Silence.* MILDRED *and* NORMAN *leave.* BOBBY *and* LORETTA *are together. He touches her.*]

BOBBY   I won't let'm hurt ya. I won't ever let'm hurt ya.

            [LORETTA *looks at* BOBBY. *A beat, she then looks at* MICKEY *waking up. She is an adult. She and* BOBBY *look at each other and then away.* BOBBY *stands up and moves to one side.* LORETTA *bends over* MICKEY {1980}.]

LORETTA   When most babies are born, they cry and cry —
           but you just cried a minute. They wiped ya all
           off and brought ya to me — I can't even tell ya
           how pretty ya smelled, how pink ya looked.
           (Beat) When I get mad, it's not because I don't
           love ya — 'cause I do, I do. It's not because I
           don't love ya.

           [LORETTA *carries* MICKEY *back to the kitchen
           area and* BOBBY. MICKEY *falls asleep in her
           arms.*]

LORETTA   Can you tell Mickey that you won't teach him
           to box? I think that would be the best way.

BOBBY   Yeah, sure. *(Beat)* Boxin is ...

LORETTA   Yeah?

BOBBY   It isn't always bad.

LORETTA   No?

BOBBY   Teaches a man self respect.

LORETTA   Mickey's not a man, he's a little boy.

BOBBY   Right. You think Mom's right? He looks like
           me?

LORETTA   Yeah. *(Beat)* The boat people. They move
           halfway across the world to escape Christ only
           knows what hell, only to have people fight
           about whether they'll play bingo in English or
           French.

BOBBY   Kind a funny, ain't it?

LORETTA   No.

BOBBY   *(Beat)* Sometimes, I mean ... when Mom talks about the French and that, she don't think sometimes.

LORETTA   She never did. *(Beat)* She phoned me, ya know, just before you got out. Said you were a good boxer.

BOBBY   Yeah, well ...

LORETTA   Said you won a medal or somethin'.

BOBBY   I guess. *(Beat)* Gets pretty rough down there, ya know. Ya got a ... I donno ... Ya got a fight to keep your head above water.

LORETTA   Sink'r swim.

BOBBY   Yeah, I guess. *(Beat)* When you're all at the bottom, ya still fight with each other 'bout who's lower, ya know? Me fightin' it out with some Frenchman from Moncton 'bout who's better. Punchin' the hell out a each other. But that's not what it's about. Boxin'.

LORETTA   No?

BOBBY   No. *(Beat)* S'not about him — the other guy. S'bout you, ya know. Me. S'about movin', s'about doin' somethin', s'about ... *(He shrugs.)* S'about me.

SCENE TEN

[MILDRED *appears by herself in moonlight wearing a nightgown and Norman's coat {1980}.*]

MILDRED   I used to think about this so much, about somethin' happenin' to ya. When you're out with Romeo and the boys, I'd think to myself, "I just hope he gets so good and drunk he falls right off that wharf." I could even imagine this damned old coat of yours gettin' heavy with water and haulin' ya under. Imagined it so strong I could smell it, smell a waterlogged old coat, hear it drippin' on the kitchen floor. I could even picture ya stretched out on the table. I practiced what I'd say to Reverend Lewis when I phoned to tell him. By then I'd have myself so worked up that I'd sit up half the night and wait for ya to come in. And when ya did I'd be so goddam mad for makin' me go through this night after night, so goddam mad I'd bite your head off. *(Beat)* So now it's gone and happened. *(Beat)* I wish I could say I'm sorry. But I'm a poor Christian. I'm a damn poor excuse for a Christian.

SCENE ELEVEN

[LORETTA *goes to* BENOIT *in Montreal bedroom. He holds the blouse she threw at him in scene seven.*]

LORETTA   You want some tea?

[BENOIT *shakes his head.*]

I should finish packing.

[*She looks at him — he doesn't move. During the scene he will hand her the blouse.*]

When Mom phoned this morning to tell me bout Dad, I was still asleep — just after you left — and I must've been dreamin' bout Louis Hebert, 'cause for a minute it all got mixed up in my head. We were on this old fashioned ship — with sails — and then all of a sudden I'm talkin' to Mom. *(Beat)* Oh Benny. I've gone and ruined everything.

BENOIT   *(Very softly, almost to himself:)* I am not him, mais je suis mort. You killed me. I'm dead, I'm a dead man.

[*He backs slowly away as lights fade out on him.* LORETTA *lowers her head, then goes to* BOBBY *{1980}.*]

SCENE TWELVE

[BOBBY *and* LORETTA *on the beach {1980}.*]

LORETTA   You gonna stay at Mom's?

BOBBY   Just till she gets squared away. Al LeBlanc at the garage? He's got a place downshore I think I'll take.

LORETTA   Good.

BOBBY   Yeah. She's got a stand on her own, ya know. She shouldn't need me so much.

LORETTA   She just wants you to love her.

179

BOBBY   That she does. She's got herself right out in front.

               [MICKEY *runs onto the beach a distance behind them, playing. They look at him and wave. He waves back, then does a pratfall for them. They laugh and watch him as they talk.*]

LORETTA   You going out with anybody?

BOBBY   No. One a the guy's I's in Dorchester with has a sister. We just, ya know *(Shrugs)* nothin'.

LORETTA   *(Beat)* You think about it much? That time you were in Dorchester?

BOBBY   What a ya think?

LORETTA   Every day.

BOBBY   Every hour a every day's more like it. When I's there, I dreams all a time bout gettin' out. Like flyin' dreams over the woods. Now I'm out and every time I go to sleep I can't stop dreamin' bout bein' stuck back there. Friggin' nightmares.

               [MICKEY *runs off, playing further up the beach.* LORETTA *watches him as he leaves. Then, she and* BOBBY *are alone.*]

LORETTA   God, it's beautiful here. So, so beautiful.

BOBBY   Yeah.

LORETTA   It's almost nicer like this — I mean, in the fall with no tourists. All ours.

BOBBY   Right. *(Beat)* This is the place, right here.

LORETTA   What?

BOBBY   Where it happened.

LORETTA   Here?

BOBBY   Just out there.

LORETTA   I always thought it was down that way, closer to where the beach house used to be.

BOBBY   No. It was here. 'Course, it's all different now. Sands changed and dune used a be bigger. And it happened out there on the second sand bar. Tide's way out that night and just startin' to come back.

LORETTA   I thought it happened over there by the big dune.

BOBBY   Nope.

LORETTA   Mike Vatour who worked over at the canteen, remember? He took kids over there next day, showed them blood on the sand.

BOBBY   Any blood would a been washed away by the tide.

LORETTA   Oh.

BOBBY   It happened out there — fifty, sixty feet. Blood's all out there. Tide's high today, eh? Fall tide. *(Beat)* Dad killed a guy once, in the war.

181

LORETTA   Yeah?

BOBBY   Nightmares all his life he told me. Remember he used a holler in his sleep, we used a laugh at him, make fun of it?

LORETTA   We were just kids. We didn't know.

BOBBY   Right.

LORETTA   Poor Dad. *(Beat)* You ever ... a ... dream about Louis?

BOBBY   Sometimes. I remember one time I dreamed bout him when I was still back there. We're little kids, like before school and that. And we're goin' to visit you and Jossette in Montreal on the train. Didn't make sense. Don't sound scary, but it was.

LORETTA   I bet.

BOBBY   I seen Jossette once.

LORETTA   Yeah?

BOBBY   Yeah. In Moncton. I saw her at the Highfield Square Mall buyin' her kid a doughnut. Down at the Food Fair.

LORETTA   She see you?

BOBBY   No. I didn't know what to do. I didn't know what to say and I wanted to say somethin'. But what? There's nothin' big enough to say. I had to run into the bathroom there, be sick. It just come over me like that, like all a sudden I got a throw my guts up.

LORETTA So she didn't see you?

BOBBY Pretty sure.

LORETTA How's she look?

BOBBY She's fat, like her mother. That's how come I knew it was her. I thought it was Mrs. Hebert, but she's too young lookin'. She looked like her mom when we was all kids.

LORETTA She looks like her Mom! Jeese, poor Jossette. That's a fate worse'n death.

BOBBY I was so scared a runnin' into her, of runnin' into anybody. I mean, even after all that time when I's in Dorchester. But now I seen her, it's not so bad. *(Beat)* I know some guys who're in with me, ya know, for murder, first degree, and one a them, guy named Ricky, s'like nothin' to him. Ricky's got no conscience, nothin'.. Water off a duck's back. And I used a think, "Boys, pretty great to be like that" type a thing. Not to see it over and over, feel bad over and over. But that guy, I donno, like he's got a big piece missin' inside, ya know? Ricky ain't all there. And it's no good wishin' I could forget, cause ya can't forget, you're not supposed to forget, see?

LORETTA I guess.

BOBBY Somethin' like that got a stay with ya all a time. I see Louis's face every day. Lyin' down there with that look on it.

LORETTA What look?

BOBBY   That I'm smarter'n-you-look. I can't even remember him lookin' scared or upset or anythin'. But he must a. All's I can remember's that friggin' smug look on him, lookin' up at me like I's a piece a trash. And I just kept kickin' him cause I knew he was right.

LORETTA   No.

BOBBY   Yeah, I got so mad cause he was right. I just kept kickin'm. Don't matter I was drunk. I knew I was kickin'm. I knows that's the worse thing I ever did. But if I forgets about it, then it's even more terrible. And I'm like Ricky. Somethin' big missin' inside.

LORETTA   Oh, jeese, Bobby.

[*They walk a bit, awkward, not touching.*]

LORETTA   Benoit and I've split up.

BOBBY   Oh.

LORETTA   Yeah. Don't tell Mom yet.

BOBBY   No.

[*She sits down on the sand. A beat and he sits a couple of feet from her.*]

LORETTA   I left him.

BOBBY   *(Beat)* Did he —

LORETTA   I hurt him. I hurt him real bad.

BOBBY   *(Beat)* Oh.

LORETTA   *(Beat)* I guess sometimes the only way we get through something awful is, I don't know, by doing something just as bad. I'm sorry Bobby.

BOBBY   Me too, Sis.

              [*They can't look at each other. The sound of waves grows slowly louder until the end of the play. After a moment* LORETTA *starts very quietly to sing.*]

LORETTA   Lipstick on your collar
              Told a tale on yo-ou
              Lipstick on your collar
              Said you were untrue
              Bet your bottom dollar
              You and I are through
              Cause lipstick on your ...

              [*They look at each other and smile. Then they look away and sit very still. There is nothing but the sound of the waves.*]

Fathers and Sons

For Doug Guildford

Cast:

HILT
ALLEN
HELENA

Although Hilt and Allen are father and son, they should be played by actors who are approximately the same age. Helena is a musician's role (Baroque violinist).

The set should be as simple as possible to allow for easy transitions. The props (chairs, cot, etc.) are uncluttered, easily moved and used in a playful way.

The play is in four sections which are linked by Biber's Mystery Sonata No. 5 in A major. Each of the four sections is staged with no breaks between scenes.

"Fathers and Sons" was workshopped at the 1998 Banff PlayRites Colony.

The play was first produced by the Tarragon Theatre, Toronto on October 20, 1998.

Cast:
Hilt	Andrew Massingham
Allen	Hume Baugh
Helena	Laurel Mascarenhas

Set and lights	Glenn Davidson
Costumes	Michelle Smith
Stage Manager	Bea Campbell

Directed by Don Hannah

ONE

MY BOY AND HIS DOG

[*A chair for* HILT. *A blanket, a bicycle for* ALLEN].

[*As the lights go down, a violin is heard playing the first seven bars from the Prelude of Biber's Mystery Sonata No. 5 in A major.*]

1. The Little World

HILT   The first word he said was "Mama."

ALLEN   Maam.

HILT   I came home from work and Mary said, "Listen!"

ALLEN   Maam.

HILT   Of course he'd say her name first. I have to say I envied her just a wee bit for being able to stay home with him.

ALLEN   Maama.

HILT   Sometimes, at the office, maybe when I was having my lunch, I'd think of them at home together.

ALLEN   Maam. Maama.

HILT   Not that I had a lot of time to sit around and think.

ALLEN   Oggie.

HILT   For awhile there, it seemed that every night when I came home they had something new to show me.

ALLEN   Oggie.

HILT   Doggie?

ALLEN   Oggie oggie addie.

HILT   Our dog.

ALLEN   Addie.

HILT   Laddie. Laddie was jealous at first, but they became best friends. When Mary set the playpen up in the living room, Laddie left his blanket in the kitchen and began to sleep beside it. He would look up and growl if he didn't like the way we played with the baby.

ALLEN   Addie oggie. Ingle. Ingle ingle.

HILT   His favourite song. *(Sings:)* "Twinkle twinkle little star, How I wonder what you are ..."

ALLEN   Ingle ingle. Ingle ingle. Awl. Awlie.

HILT   His ball. Bouncie, bouncie?

ALLEN   Awl. *(Giggles:)* Ounce ounce.

HILT   I loved those foolish words. They described his whole world, so small and safe. His playpen, his toys, his mother, Laddie.

I left that little world every morning when Bert Seaman's Oldsmobile pulled up in front of the house to take me to work.

Cold this morning.

Bert's wife Olive would bring their baby over in the afternoon sometimes. Made me mad. Well, it was hard on Mary. Besides, she knew that Bert was having an affair with a girl at the office, Margaret Tate. At work, Bert always called her Miss Tate, except to me. Whenever he talked to me, he called her Peggy. I knew that he knew that I knew all about, well, the goings-on. He never mentioned it, but it was understood that if I wanted to keep my job I would have to be some kind of accomplice.

When he talked about Olive, he never used her name, not once. Olive's name was The Wife.

That's right Bert, freeze the balls off a brass monkey.

Not too bad, yourself? How's The Wife?

ALLEN   Ad addie ad!

HILT   Dad, Daddy, Lad and Laddie. My name sounded the same to me as Laddie's, who slept beside the playpen, who guarded the crib. Who lay there patiently while Allen crawled all over him, mauled him.

ALLEN   Addie ad! Addie ad!

HILT   Careful! Don't hurt him. He might snap at you.

192

ALLEN   Addie ad!

HILT   Only his mother could tell when he meant me
               and when he meant the dog.

ALLEN   Addie ad.

HILT   He began to walk. He spoke his first sentence.

ALLEN   Me addie ad co auk.

HILT   On Sundays, after church, Mary would go over
               to her sister's while we went for walks up and
               down the street: my son, my dog and me. My
               own father had never done such a thing. He was
               distant — well, ye gods, the man was
               handicapped.

               Mary used to thank me for letting her visit
               Gladys, for giving her a break from the baby,
               but it was my favourite time. Just walking down
               to Main Street then back up past the house to
               the end of the pavement, then back down again.
               Up and down. Pushing the pram. Then carrying
               him. Then holding his hand.

               Tree.

ALLEN   Reee reee.

HILT   Ditch.

ALLEN   Itch itchy.

HILT   Swing.

ALLEN   Up wing up.

HILT   But every weekday morning at seven-thirty, I was driven away from all these things.

             Not too bad. Not so cold this morning.

             How's The Wife?

             Bert was always bragging about his kid, but I never talked to him about my boy. I didn't even want to mention Allen's name while I was in that car.

ALLEN   Ingle ingle ito car ...

HILT   Each night, after she put Allen to bed, read him a story, Mary would ask me how things went at work. It didn't seem right to drag her into it, but I had to get it off my chest, I suppose. Bert was drinking, and a big part of my job, and Margaret's job too, was spent trying to cover for him. Poor Margaret, I felt sorry for her. She believed that one day Bert would leave The Wife, stop drinking, and marry her.

             "So how'd it go today?" Mary would ask.

             Oh, alright. It was alright.

             "Doesn't sound like it to me," she'd say. We'd be doing the dishes. Laddie would be outside in the evening chasing something around the yard. Neighbours' cat. A porcupine. His tail.

             Crazy dog.

ALLEN   Aanie, maanie, maanie ...

HILT   "He's just talking himself to sleep," she'd say. "How'd it go?"

> *I don't know, I just don't know.*

> *Well, Bert took Margaret out for lunch and they didn't get back till after four. Old Gunther was down from Montreal and I didn't have a clue where the payroll report was. Bert didn't tell me, Margaret didn't say a word about it. No one told me the man was coming. So there I was covering for the two of them while they're off in a goddam motel room somewhere and Gunther's acting like I don't know how to do my job. Goddamn payroll report has nothing to do with me, but can I say that to him? No. So I go into Bert's filing cabinet but there's not a damn thing in there but goddam Seagram's bottles. The man's nothing but a damn booze artist.*

Then Mary tells me that Olive dropped by with that screaming brat of their's and dumped him here while she went over to Dorca's to get her hair done.

ALLEN   *(Gurgles and mumbles in his sleep.)*

HILT   Before we went to bed, we'd stand at his bedroom door and watch him sleep.

ALLEN   *(Gurgles, mumbles.)*

HILT   When Mary told me that she was pregnant again, she said, "How will we ever manage?" Money was tight, but we could manage. I was so happy. I thought, "We can go on and on like this forever."

2. Bicycle

[ALLEN *rides a bicycle in circles around his father. He becomes more and more assured, cocky.*]

ALLEN   Lookit me! Lookit me!

HILT   Careful! Be careful!

My father wasn't born blind — he had a terrible accident when he was five. Cutting a knot out of a shoelace when the scissors slipped. Infection spread from the punctured eye to the other one — he lost them both.

I grew up with this story but it never made me queasy until after the boys were born.

Dad went away to the School for the Blind and studied music.

Everybody respected him. He tuned their pianos. They used to say, "If you were to drop old Fred off on any street corner in town, he'd find his way home." And it was true. His father, my grandfather, was a carpenter, cabinet maker — he built most of the cottages down here along the shore. He would give my father the dimensions for the cottage, then Dad would do the calculations in his head. "You'll need so many two by fours," he'd say, "And this much planking and so many pounds of nails and bundles of shingles" and so forth. And boys-oh-boys, when that cottage was finished, you could cart off all that was left over in a wheelbarrow. He was a smart man.

When he went on a rampage, Mom would hide with me behind the chesterfield and try to pretend it was a game.

But his ears were so goddam sharp —

[ALLEN *nearly drives into his father.*]

HILT Be careful! Ye gods man, watch where you're going!

3. Dollars and Cents

ALLEN Can I have a couple of dollars?

HILT Allen my boy, I'm sorry to say I don't have it.

ALLEN Just a couple of dollars.

HILT I said "I don't have it," I'm sorry.

ALLEN Just a dollar.

HILT Are you deaf?

ALLEN I won't waste it.

HILT I never said you would.

ALLEN Just a dollar.

HILT Allen!

197

ALLEN   It's no fair.

HILT   Don't talk to me about fair.

ALLEN   Billy Seaman's dad gives him money whenever he wants it.

HILT   Yeah, well, Billy Seaman's father makes more money than yours does.

ALLEN   Just a couple of dollars.

HILT   Quit hounding me for money you know I don't have.

ALLEN   Billy Seaman's dad lets him stay up and watch "Route 66." He gave him a three-speed bike. Why are you so mean?

HILT   Boys-oh-boys, you're cruisin' for a bruisin' there, buster.

ALLEN   Just a crummy dollar.

HILT   I'm sorry but no, and that's final.

ALLEN   (Cheapskate.)

HILT   Go to your room.

ALLEN   Fifty cents. Fifty measly cents.

HILT   Are you deaf? I said, "Go to your room!"

ALLEN   I hate you.

HILT   *I saw that Seaman kid down at the*

wharf. What a sad, miserable looking kid. Does he ever go home? Well, why would he? Olive sitting at a card table in the living room all day long playing solitaire and pouring back the gin. Bert out fishing with one of his cronies from the Lion's Club. Poor Margaret.

So there's Billy Seaman today down at the wharf all by himself. He's skipping silver dollars, fifty cent pieces out into the bay. Like they were stones he picked up on the beach. Saddest damn thing you ever saw. "Hi, Billy," I says, and he just glares at me and shrugs.

Saddest damn thing you ever saw.

4. Movies

ALLEN   I don't hafta go! You can't make me!

HILT   Olive phoned me up the day after it happened and asked me if I'd be a pallbearer. Mary says to me, "The old So-and-So's dead and you're still luggin' his useless arse around for him."

ALLEN   No fair. We're supposed to go to Fundy Park today! You promised!

HILT   I can't say I was sorry to see old Bert go. Terrible isn't it? Not very Christian of me. Heart attack in the parking lot of Keddy's Motor Lodge. Poor Margaret.

ALLEN   I'm old enough to stay home by myself. Bobby

just wants to go because he's stupid. I don't wanna see some old dead body.

HILT   Holy-gods-a-war, what a show that was!

ALLEN   Why do I hafta shine my shoes? No one's gonna look at my feet. Not when there's a dead body to look at.

HILT   "When I go," I says to Mary, "When I go, for the love-a-god I want nothing like that!" Weepin', carryin' on — Olive three sheets to the wind wailing about what a great humanitarian poor Bert was, cut down in his prime, Loving Father, the greatest husband a wife could want — Blah, blah, blah. And poor Margaret at the back of the church in that damn navy blue dress Bert bought her when they went to Montreal last year on "business." Bert's brother, that useless tit of an arsehole, running around with a goddam movie camera capturing the whole thing for posterity. He's up and down like a bride's drawers through the whole miserable exercise. And every damn kid there starts waving like a fool everytime he points it their way.

ALLEN   It's no fair you wouldn't let me be in the movie! You never let me do anything!

HILT   Go to your room!

        Poor Billy Seaman. But there's not a damn thing you can do.

200

5. Virgins

ALLEN   Do virgins only come at Christmas time?

HILT   What?

ALLEN   Like Round John Virgin in "Silent Night."

HILT   It's July. What in the name-a-God are you talking about?

ALLEN   What's a virgin anyway?

HILT   Why do you want to know that?

ALLEN   It's in this book I got at the library.

HILT   I don't think you're old enough to be reading that book. You better take it back.

6. Trees

HILT   He started living in trees.

Out the door at the crack of dawn and up into one of the old maples beside the house. At first he'd use his bike, lean it against the trunk and stand on the seat so he could reach the branch. He'd stay up there all day long if we let him.

What the hell do you do up there?

ALLEN   I was reading. Is that a crime now?

HILT   No, I never said that.

If Mary or me said "Have you seen Allen?" the other one would answer "Have you checked the trees yet?"

ALLEN   I was reading. What do you want?

HILT   Reading.

When it got so he didn't need the bike, he'd lean it up against another one of the maples to fool us. I'd be standing out there under an empty tree calling for him. Dot and Maurice from next door would be over in their yard laughing at me. "Hey Hilt! You're barkin' up the wrong tree." Ha ha, very funny.

The worst of it was, I knew he was up there mostly to get away from me.

7. First Dog Story

ALLEN   Here Laddie! Here boy!

HILT   Poor dog got old and snappy.

ALLEN   Here Laddie Laddie Laddie!

HILT   It makes you wonder why people even have pets. You can't help but love the damn things and then one day you find them run over by the side of the road, or else you have to take them in to the vet and have them put out of their misery. Every story about a dog is a sad story.

ALLEN   Laddie! Here boy! C'mon!

HILT   Poor old thing was in pain. Limping around. Couldn't control his bladder. Then he nipped at little Bobby. Nothing serious, but it scared us. Mary took the boys to her sister's to see their new colour TV and I put Laddie on a blanket in the backseat of the Chev.

ALLEN   Laddie? Laddie?

HILT   Allen was old enough to understand, but that doesn't make it any easier.

     When we first got married, when I got away from Mom and Dad, I felt that I was starting a new life and that there'd be no more of the tension and upset that I had to put up with when I was a boy. I wanted none of that in my own family. We'd all be moving forwards from a clean slate. But I'm driving along with poor old Laddie stinking up the back seat of the car thinking how happy we used to be when the boys were wee things and Laddie followed them around the yard. I'm driving along and for the first time in my life I'm wishing I could turn back the clock.

8. Second Dog Story

[HILT *is lying on the floor.*]

ALLEN   Dad, Dad! Laddie can catch a ball. I threw the ball and he catched it in his teeth! Can he sleep with me tonight?

HILT   What did your mother say?

203

ALLEN   She said to ask you.

                 [*During his speech,* HILT *lifts his legs in the air and* ALLEN *leans against his feet. They hold hands.* HILT *straightens his legs, lifting* ALLEN *up into the air. They let go of each other's hands and* ALLEN *holds his outstretched. Before the speech is over,* ALLEN *scrambles back to his feet and looks down on his father.*]

HILT   Now, I know that he hasn't asked her yet because he knows what the answer will be. She doesn't want the dog on the bed, she's got rules about dog hair and beds. His plan is to run back and forth between the two of us till one of us says "yes," and he'll be more upset if it's me that says "no" because I set him off. But what the hell difference will a few dog hairs make? But then I'm not the one stuck home all day doing the washing. I want to say "yes" because it would make him happy, and all we seem to do anymore is argue and fight. But more than anything right now I want to be able to curl up beside him, and have him put his arm over me. I never want to go to that goddam office again, I want to have my boy toss me a ball so I can catch it in my teeth and run circles around the yard —

ALLEN   Can he, Dad? Can he?

                 [*They are looking at each other, both waiting for the answer, when* HELENA *begins to play the complete Prelude to Biber's Sonata No. 5 in A major. The lights fade on* ALLEN *and* HILT.]

204

TWO

THE BIRDS AND THE BEES

[*Two chairs.*]

1. Genealogy

ALLEN   Sometimes my brother and I went to Grandfather's cottage for the day.

Once Gramma emptied a new box of cereal into a mixing bowl so I could get the prize right away. A plastic frogman. You put baking soda in it then you put it in the water and it made bubbles.

Grandfather went swimming with rubber shoes on and I was always afraid that he would start swimming in the wrong direction and get lost. I was afraid that his glass eyes would fall out and water would leak into his head.

Gramma took me into the bathroom with her. She would talk to me while she sat on the toilet. I remember watching her slowly tear two pieces of toilet paper from the roll, one neat little square at a time, and place them beside each other on her knee. Bunching up a wad of toilet paper meant that you had no understanding of how people had suffered during the Great Depression.

Going to the toilet with Gramma was a lesson in good breeding.

HILT   My father only ever talked to me when he

needed something done. My mother brought up the subject of sex exactly once. She said she hoped I wouldn't be like every other man and then she pretended to cry.

2. Church Camp

ALLEN   At church camp they woke us with a bell at the crack of dawn and we ran outside to salute the flag. We washed in cold water and made bird houses out of popsicle sticks. Everyday we had Bible study, we went swimming and hiking, and every night we sang "We Are Climbing Jacob's Ladder" around the camp fire. Then, after lights out, came the best part.

Hey, I know one, I know a good one!

"Tom and Mary went to the dairy
Tom pulled out his long and hairy.
Mary said, "What a whopper,
Let's lay down and do it proper."
Two months later all was well,
Six months later began to swell
Nine months later, what a shock!
A baby was born with a six inch cock."

3. Easy Women

HILT   I don't understand men who talk about girls that way. Take Ed Folley back in high school — he used to brag to us about the things he did with Kay Ross, and I'd think, Holy-gods-a-war, he can't think much of her, talking the way he does. Then she dropped out of school in Grade

Eleven and he dropped out too because he had to marry her. I'd see them sometimes on Main Street with their kids and think, How would those kids feel if they ever found out what Ed used to say about their mother?

I never talked about Mary, never said anything personal. It was nobody's business.

The few times that my mother said personal things to me about Dad, it seemed that she was asking me to choose between them.

The only person I could ever talk to was Mary.

What did they have against Mary?

ALLEN   Brenda Mullins didn't live in a house, she lived in an apartment over a store with her divorced mother which made her sophisticated and worldly. She smelled differently from the other girls in Grade Nine — sweaty, fleshy. She walked fast, always looked straight ahead, and her favourite word was "screw." She invited me back to her apartment one day after school. We told dirty jokes all the way up Church Street and I wondered if I would get to screw her. But her mother was home so we just drank Cokes and watched TV. When I was leaving, Brenda gave me a dirty book that she had stolen from her mother's boyfriend. "Small Town Swap Set."

It was the most exciting thing I had ever read, and it felt so much safer than actually dealing with a real girl like Brenda. I loved reading it. The excitement of seeing the word "tits." It gave me such a thrill to see it written, to see the letters "T-I-T-S" in a sentence on the page.

4. More Genealogy

HILT

Mary and I never fought. But every time we did, it was about my mother. And the worst was awful. It was hot all that spring and Mary was pregnant again and sick all the time. And it seemed that Mom needed me whenever I turned around. To take off the storm windows, to clean up the yard, to move them out to the cottage for the summer.

The day after I moved them was the hottest day I've ever known. Mary was in the hospital, in labour, and Mom wanted me to rearrange the cottage, make room for my old crib so we could bring the new baby down. Bobby was asleep on a blanket in the shade and Allen and Mom were playing "Go Fish" on the veranda. Dad was out in a lawnchair reading the Braille Gospels. There wasn't a phone at the cottage.

Late in the afternoon, Gladys arrived to tell me that Mary had lost the baby.

5. Rhymes

ALLEN

Connie Barnes was a year older than me and she asked me to a party at her cousin's cottage. It was a rainy night and pretty soon we were on top of a bed necking. The nearness of her frightened me. She was short and plump and flat chested and I liked talking to her. But her tongue in my mouth made me really uncomfortable; she seemed to be the sort of girl that only would be doing this if we were serious. And I knew we weren't.

In the next room, her cousin had taken the Rolling Stones off the stereo and was playing the soundtrack to "Dr. Zhivago." Everybody had paired off and we were all necking and the classy music was supposed to make the girls feel that they weren't doing anything cheap.

Although neither one of us wanted to see the other after that night, I wrote a very long poem about how lonely I was without Connie. The last line of each stanza was "Lying alone without my muse." It was a challenge because I had to find sophisticated rhymes for "muse."

choose

blues

snooze

cruise

booze

ooze

6. Degree Work

HILT   A Freemason, therefore, should be a man of honour and conscience, preferring his duty to everything, even to his life, independent in his

209

opinions, and of good morals, submissive to the laws, devoted to humanity, his country, his family, kind and indulgent to his brethren, friend of all virtuous men, and ready and willing to assist his fellows by every means in his power. Thus you will be faithful to your country, to your fellows and to God, and thus will you do honour to the name and rank of Secret Master, which, like other Masonic titles, degrades if it is not deserved.

7. At the Pope's Palace

ALLEN

Most noon hours, I left the lunch room and went for a walk by myself. I had discovered the dirty book rack at Keating's Tobacco Store.

Ones with titles like "Back Street Chippie" and "Bikers' Girl" made me uneasy. They were always set in small towns like mine and, although I tried to imagine bedrooms with silk sheets and bearskin rugs, the characters always ended up making out in the houses that I knew, in bedrooms that looked like Billy Seaman's or my parents'. It was wrong that sex — that kind of sex where women panted and screamed "Give it to me!" or two men would end up in bed with one woman, or two women with one man, or an assortment of half a dozen at an orgy in someone's living room where the women all had lipstick on their nipples — it was wrong for that kind of sex to take place in my house or the houses of my friends. It made me guilty.

But then I read "Fanny Hill" and found a whole new world of sex set in an extravagant, historical past. There was no danger of my mind wandering into Mom and Dad's room in the middle of "The Lust of Lucrezia Borgia" or "Sex Slaves of the Caesars." Time and geography saved me from the embarrassment of having Olive Seaman's love seat or my mother's brassiere turn up and ruin Caesar Borgia's orgy with fallen nuns at the Pope's Palace. Because once the offending, familiar object did arrive, it stayed in the foreground, as if my parents had put it there to remind me that what I was doing was terribly, terribly wrong.

But after a while, those places seemed so remote, so far from me, that I worried about my chances of ever getting laid. If I had the safety of history, maybe I could dispense with remote geography. I began to imagine sexy stories set in the woods around our town: lusty settlers, eager Indian braves, well stacked nymphomaniacs fresh off the boat from the castles of the old world. I knew that these books couldn't possibly exist, yet I fantasized about them and finally, when I was fourteen, I decided to write them myself.

8. Growing Up

HILT

When Mom died, suddenly there was nothing between me and Dad. No buffer, I mean.

He never smiled. He had a funny kind of laugh, kind of like "pah!"

Blind people like Dad can't smile. I think you only smile if you can see someone else doing it.

211

He started getting confused when he was out tuning pianos. I'd be getting phone calls from people to come and pick him up. He'd be walking into things, swearing. One time he fell down and thought he was at home. When the poor woman tried to help him, he tried to order her out of her own house.

9. New World

ALLEN "Tamara missed her life in London, the parties at the Duke's palace where she had been screwed by so many studly coachmen, but the moment she saw the Indian scout stand naked beside the spruce trees outside her cabin, the nipples of her tits went hard with lust. They walked slowly towards each other. His monstrous phallus started to swell and grow as he watched her big tits jiggle."

10. Birds and Bees

HILT "I want you to have a talk with him," Mary said. "I found some books under his mattress." How in the name-a-God did this happen?

I want to have a word with you.

ALLEN Yeah.

HILT *(Beat)* Your mother's very upset.

ALLEN Yeah? What happened?

HILT You know very well. It's about the things, the

books. She was spring cleaning the other day and found ...

ALLEN   Oh.

HILT   She's worried.

ALLEN   There's nothing to worry about.

HILT   She seems to think there is.

ALLEN   Well, there isn't.

HILT   *(Beat)* The way I see it, it's an expression of love between a man and a woman. It's only dirty when you make it dirty.

ALLEN   Yeah.

HILT   Do you want to end up like your cousin Larry?

ALLEN   What?

HILT   Kicked out of every school in the county. Ye gods man, you think he's going to the Baptist Training School because he's a Baptist? They're the only ones that'll have him now. *(Beat)* That little Horsman girl, they live on this side of Sunny Brae ...

ALLEN   *(Beat)* Sherri.

HILT   That's right, thank-you. Sherri Horsman's family went to see your Aunt Gladys and threatened to call the police if he didn't leave her alone.

ALLEN   I know.

HILT   Because Larry kept grabbing her — *(Beat)* her breasts — the poor girl was terrified. He followed her all over the city.

ALLEN   I know.

HILT   You want to end up like that?

ALLEN   No.

HILT   Your mother's worried.

ALLEN   There's no need to be worried.

HILT   *(Beat)* That girl, the one you went to the party with that time.

ALLEN   *(Beat)* What about her?

HILT   She's a good girl?

ALLEN   I guess, I don't know.

HILT   You don't *know?*

ALLEN   It was one party. I didn't ask her.

HILT   *(Beat)* Because your Aunt Gladys told your mother that the Horsman girl has a bit of a reputation.

ALLEN   So does Larry.

HILT   I'm not excusing your cousin. I'm only saying that you can't be too careful. *(Beat)* And I wish you'd steer clear of Billy Seaman.

214

ALLEN   The only time I see Billy is on the bus. And if I
         don't take the bus I can't go to school.

HILT   He's getting messed up with the wrong people.
         They say he's getting messed up with drugs.

ALLEN   I don't hang around with Billy.

HILT   *(Beat)* Your mother and I did our best. *(Beat)* It
         wasn't always easy. Neither one of us were born
         with a silver spoon in our mouth. *(Beat)* It's
         only natural for your mother to worry. *(Beat)*
         You read too damn many books.

ALLEN   Is reading a crime?

HILT   Every cent you get, its the only thing you buy.
         Books. Books and more books. Books and
         records. You drive your mother crazy with that
         music. Leonard Cohen and that damn Buffy
         Sainte-Marie. You call that singing?

ALLEN   Don't start up on how great Glenn Miller used
         to be. Because Grandfather hated Glenn Miller,
         you told me that. You had your music, I've got
         mine.

HILT   Lot of goddam noise. And I don't know what
         kind of books you're reading, where you get
         these ideas.

ALLEN   Reading isn't a crime.

HILT   I never said it was. But I don't approve of thinking
         about women that way. It's only dirty if you make
         it dirty. *(Beat)* I don't know. *(Beat)* Ye gods man
         — have a little respect for your mother!

215

ALLEN   It has nothing to do with Mom.

HILT   She's a woman isn't she? *(Beat)* Your mother's
             worried. She's always been grateful that you kids
             weren't like her sister's. Your cousin Larry and
             that screechy sister of his. Have you seen Nean's
             bedroom? Your Aunt Gladys let her paint
             goddam polka dots all over the walls and
             ceiling! It's a disgrace. *(Beat)* I'd be ashamed to
             have anyone come into the house and see it.
             (Beat) I never thought the day would come
             when I'd be ashamed of my own kids. *(Beat)*
             And reading that filthy trash is bad enough, but
             writing it — Holy-gods-a-war! *(Beat)* Now your
             mother was thinking that maybe you should
             talk to someone.

ALLEN   *(Beat)* Like who?

HILT   She's heard that the new minister at Central is
             good with teenagers. Your Aunt Gladys took
             Larry to see him.

ALLEN   Before or after he grabbed Sherri Horsman's
             breasts?

HILT   Don't get lippy! *(Beat)* Now, I don't think that
             sort of thing is necessary. I don't think there's
             any need of this going beyond these four walls.
             (Beat) And you know that your mother would
             only think of such a thing because she cares
             about you. *(Beat)* She's worried sick. *(Beat)* I
             think we're perfectly capable of dealing with this
             problem without any outside interference.

ALLEN   Okay.

HILT   *(Beat)* When your mother and I got married, we were — *(Beat)* We'd never done any of that. Well, I hope to God that no one I know ever does the kind of things that you ... *(Beat)* But we had done nothing to be ashamed of. Because we loved each other. *(Beat)* It all boils down to respect. Something there's too little of these days. Wild music. Drugs. We'd never even heard of such a thing. Only time you ever heard about drugs was if you went to a sleazy cops and robbers show at the old Empress. You want to end up like Billy Seaman? Cause he'll be doing time in reform school as sure as shootin'.

            [ALLEN *rolls his eyes.*]

HILT   You will never have anything to do with that kind of trash again. Is that understood?

ALLEN   Yes.

HILT   I wish I could believe you, but your mother and I can't trust you anymore. *(Beat)* But for now, the subject is closed. And I hope to God there's no reason for us ever to talk about this sort of thing again.

            [*They are looking away from each other as the lights on them go out and come up on* HELENA *as she plays the Allemande of Biber's Sonata No. 5 in A major.*]

217

THREE

MY FATHER'S AGE

[*A cot for* HILT. *A chair or stool for* ALLEN.]

1. Circuses

ALLEN   Every Saturday morning my brother and I were stuck in the back seat of the old Chev when my parents drove the twenty miles into town to buy groceries.

HILT   You two knock it off or you'll find yourselves walking home!

ALLEN   When we passed Sunny Brae and drove over the little bridge at Hall's Creek, I would look out the back seat windows at what was left of the old stadium. It was just a shell, round and grey — it had arches. There had been a fire long before I was born.

HILT   I wasn't much older than you when the whole thing went up in flames.

ALLEN   It was a ruin as glamorous to me as the Coliseum in the Encyclopedia. Whenever Dad spoke about playing hockey when he was a kid —

HILT   With rolled up newspapers for shin pads — none of that fancy equipment like you kids have today.

ALLEN   I imagined those games taking place in that stadium, my father playing hockey like a gladiator in ancient Rome. Before I was five,

218

my father's boyhood was far away and glamorous. Close by the stadium were the fields where the circuses of my father's boyhood set up their big tents.

HILT   Circus had its own train back then. We boys'd run down to the tracks just to see her come in.

ALLEN   The only black man that my father ever talked about came to town with the circus. Dad and his friends were watching the big top go up —

HILT   There were lions and elephants — all kinds of animals — and that fella was right in the middle of it all, pounding in those tent pegs with a mallet as big as you are. Boys he was big — must have been six and a half feet tall and he had shoulders on him like a bear.

ALLEN   There was an ancient city ordinance prohibiting Negroes from being in town after sunset. Did they make an exception for him? Did the circus people hide him after dark? Did he have to sleep in the woods?

HILT   He just walloped those pegs in — boys-oh-boys, like sticks into butter!

ALLEN   I don't know the first time I heard this story

HILT   Me and the boys watched him from the distance. His arms were like Popeye the sailorman's — as big around as your waist!

ALLEN   That black man was more exotic to me than the elephants, than the lions in cages, than the ladies on horseback. I had never heard my father speak of anyone or anything with such awe.

HILT   Boys-oh-boys, he was one *enormous* coon.

ALLEN   I was taken to my own circus one miserably hot and muggy summer afternoon when I was four or five. I remember being confused and frightened because a fat lady sat on me in the bleachers then she said something mean — she was a stranger and then suddenly she was mad at me because she had crushed the wind out of me. There were acrobats and trapeze artists and wild animals but mostly I remember that it was too hot and it was out by the new overpass and not near the stadium and that somehow this was wrong and I was not being allowed to see the circus of my father. Somehow I had failed him again.

In my father's circus, elephants trumpeted in the air with the silhouette of the old stadium behind them. When I think of that picture, it is raining violently, animals are straining at their ropes, the air is filled with cries and confusion, and standing huge and in the midst of it all is the only black man I ever heard my father tell a story about. He slams down that mallet over and over bringing order to the chaos. When he is finished, the circus is in place.

2. Margarine

ALLEN   There was a butter lobby in New Brunswick when I was a kid.

HILT   What the hell is wrong with the government?

ALLEN   Dairy farmers would have been happy to totally ban margarine but they could not.

HILT   Last time I looked this was a free country. When the hell are they going to start looking out for the little guy?

ALLEN   For awhile, the only margarine we could buy was pale and lard like.

HILT   Goddam government.

ALLEN   Coloured margarine was talked about in our house like a miracle substance. Dad pronounced it like this:

HILT &
ALLEN   Marjean.

ALLEN   like an exotic southern girl.

HILT   That marjean's good as butter any day. No sir, ya can't beat it for the price.

ALLEN   It was unfair that we were not allowed to buy coloured margarine while the citizens of nearby Nova Scotia could.

HILT   Let's take a drive over to Amherst and get some of that coloured marjean. Goddam government.

ALLEN   Back then it was a couple of hours drive. One of the wonders of the town of Amherst was that there were black people living there.

HILT   They came up from the States on the
            underground railway.

ALLEN   I imagined black people crowded into little coal
            cars like miners, driving for days under ceilings
            of stalactites. When can we take the
            underground railway?

HILT   Don't talk foolish.

ALLEN   There were whole families of them living in
            Amherst. My father would slow down the car and
            we would look at black children on the sidewalk,
            playing hopscotch and skipping rope. My mother
            would say, "You can look at them, but for
            godsakes don't gawk." Their hair fascinated us.

HILT   It's bristly isn't it? Like steel wool I'd imagine.

ALLEN   My mother would brush away his remark with
            her hand. "Oh, Hilt, it is not! It's soft like a
            little lamb's."

HILT   Ye gods woman.

ALLEN   If one of the children ever looked our way, my
            mother would say, "Oh, look at that little
            piccaninny! Couldn't you just take her home!"

HILT   Ye gods woman!

ALLEN   Sometimes I would see black people in the
            supermarket. I remember one large, bored
            looking woman pushing her cart ahead of us. At
            the dairy case, I was shocked to see her pick up
            two pounds of butter. She was buying what we
            had come all this way to avoid.

222

HILT   She must be made-a-money that one.

3. Ice

ALLEN   The first black person I ever talked to was a girl in first year university. Her name was Venise and she was from Trinidad and I told her I would take her for her first walk on ice. There was a little pond in the centre of campus; on Tuesdays and Thursdays as we walked from English 101 we watched it slowly freeze over. One Saturday morning, we met at the pond. "It will break, I know," she said. "I'll fall through, I'll fall through!" We inched our way out to the middle — both of us were laughing but she was shaking from fear. The surface was smooth and clear, with just a trace of little ripples. "Soul on Ice," she said, but she was too nervous for it to be really funny. I was thinking that, unlike my parents, I was living in a brave new world where I could know black people, where I might even have a black girlfriend. Unlike my father —

HILT   What's wrong with getting a Bachelor in Commerce?

ALLEN   who disagreed with me on everything —

HILT   What the hell have you got against making money?

ALLEN   *Unlike my father* I would never use a word like "coon." I grabbed her hand. She was the first black person I ever touched. But then, we didn't touch, really. We were both wearing mittens.

223

4. Hospital

ALLEN   The summer that Elvis died, I left New
               Brunswick for grad school. The two events were
               not related — I've never been good with dates
               and my strongest memory of driving to Ontario
               was listening to an outpouring of emotion for
               the King on the car radio. Before I left, I was
               staying with my father — my mother had been
               dragged out west with her sister on a trip that
               she did not want to take and Dad's heart was
               bad. Then the airlines went on strike and Mom
               was stranded in Moose Jaw with Aunt Gladys
               and my cousin Nean who cried hysterically
               every day and wanted to leave her husband.

HILT   That damn Nean never knew what she wanted.
               Your mother no more wanted to fly out and get
               into that mess than I want to go and jump off
               the wharf.

ALLEN   Dad and I had not gotten along particularly
               well for years and it was a tense time. I cooked
               for him, we had awkward conversations, and he
               dispensed advice. He had not been allowed to
               go to university and he believed that graduate
               school would get me a real job.

HILT   Your brother's happy.

ALLEN   Bobby is an accountant who works for his
               father-in-law. They're all Baptists. His yappy
               wife nagged the poor bastard until he put on a
               white robe and got dipped in the Petitcodiac
               River by Reverend Smiley, a man later charged
               with soliciting minors in the washroom at the
               local mall.

HILT	If you had a real job like your brother you could be happy too.
ALLEN	I had never been able to please my father.
HILT	A poet. What the hell kind of job is that?
ALLEN	On some level both of his sons had disappointed him because neither of us had been interested in Freemasonry. When we were teenagers, Dad had taken each of us aside and tried to get us to join Demolay.
HILT	You'd wear a cape in the Masonic Parade.
ALLEN	This got him nowhere. The Masonic Parade was an annual ordeal. Mention "parade" to a kid and what does he think of? Brass bands. Floats. Not the embarrassment of watching a bunch of old men walk down the middle of Main Street wearing aprons with badges on them.
HILT	Those capes have beautiful lining.
ALLEN	But what do they do in Demolay?
HILT	It's a secret organization.
ALLEN	I know, so what's it all about?
HILT	It's a secret organization.
ALLEN	I know, but can't you give me some idea? What do they do?
HILT	Are you *deaf?* It's a *secret organization.*

ALLEN   Well, how the hell can you expect me to join something when you can't tell me anything about it?

HILT   Ye gods man, it's a *secret organization!*

ALLEN   And so it went.

HILT   Don't you even want to know how to give the secret Masonic handshake?

ALLEN   If you think it's something I should know, you could just show it to me right now.

HILT   I can't, you know that. It's a *secret organization!* Can't you get that through your thick skull?

ALLEN   That summer I had sent some work to a poet I admired and received a very kind note in the mail. I showed him the note and he had no idea what to say. I can't say that he wasn't thrilled. I can't say that he was.

HILT   Wellsir.

ALLEN   I can't explain his reaction at all.

HILT   Wellsir.

ALLEN   Trying to share this with my father was like trying to understand why he stood in front of the mirror memorizing his degree work for the Lodge.

HILT   (*Mumbles memory work quietly to himself, very seriously.*)

ALLEN   We were like people visiting each other who have very little in common.

On that night, I can't remember what we had for dinner, only that he didn't eat much and I took it personally — this man would never approve of me. He went to bed early and I went to my desk to work on the last couplet of a ghazal. It was dusk when I walked by his bedroom door.

HILT   *(Moans softly.)*

ALLEN   Dad? Are you ok?

HILT   *(Quietly)* I think I'm having a heart attack.

ALLEN   Jesus.

HILT   Would you mind taking me to the hospital?

ALLEN   I'll call an ambulance!

HILT   No, don't bother. Would you mind helping me down to the car?

ALLEN   He seemed surprised that I would drive him. But the drive into town was awful. When I turned into Sunny Brae, just before the old stadium —

HILT   Slow down! Ye gods man, be careful! This is a *forty-five miles per hour speed zone!*

ALLEN   I'm only going fifty and you're having a heart attack!

HILT　　　　*Slow down for chrissakes! Slow down and live!*

ALLEN　　　I did.

HILT　　　　Where ya goin anyway — the *graveyard?*

ALLEN　　　I was scared that if we had one of our fights he'd die right there in the front seat of the car. I'd pull up to Emergency with a corpse. I'd have to phone Moose Jaw and tell my mother that I'd killed him.

　　　　　　At the hospital I took him to the desk and before I could open my mouth —

HILT　　　　I think I'm having a heart attack.

ALLEN　　　Just before they wheeled him away —

HILT　　　　You better go move the car so we won't get a ticket. Park it on West Lane — that way you won't have to pay.

ALLEN　　　I moved the car. It was a beautiful summer night. I lit a cigarette and wished that I didn't have to go back in the hospital. For years I had longed for the day when I would be grown up, independent of my father. Now, here I was, on the verge of being in charge of things and I was not very happy being an adult. I wasn't particularly good at it either.

　　　　　　I found him on a gurney in a room that I remember as being vast. It couldn't have been

HILT　　　　Now, we won't tell your mother.

228

ALLEN but somehow that room which must have been small, fluorescent — garish and drab at once — has expanded in my mind

HILT She'd just worry.

ALLEN The lighting has grown softer and although I cannot recall much of our conversation, I remember him talking to me very calmly, as if his words were a part of the soft, summer night.

HILT Why spoil her vacation? No sense causing a fuss.

ALLEN We wouldn't call my mother, we wouldn't break the speed limit, we wouldn't park illegally. I stood there thinking that my father would die without causing a ripple.

We seemed to wait for a long time.

HILT They must be busy tonight.

ALLEN The doctor on call finally came into the room. He had been dragged away from a party — that much was obvious from his clothing. He was wearing a dashiki shirt and sandals. He was a large man — tall and big and blue, blue black. Black African black. As soon as he stepped into the room my father lurched up on the gurney and stared at him, as if a current of electricity had jabbed him at the moment the black doctor walked through the door.

"Oh, no," I thought, "Oh, nonono." And all I could think of was the circus, the rain, my father's "enormous coon" pounding in the tent pegs. I thought of his conviction that black

229

people had hair like brillo pads. I was terrified that my father would say something terrible. The doctor would think we were both bigots. He was staring at my father as if he were anticipating some dreadful remark and was getting ready to counter with one of his own. Some force was moving between my father and the man and I knew that I had to get between them and intercept it. I stood up and walked towards them — I seemed to be moving slowly across a great space.

But then that huge black man extended his hand at the same moment that my father extended his white one. "Brother Hilton," he said.

HILT   Brother Mubatto. I'm very glad to see you sir.

ALLEN   Freemasons.

HILT   This is my son, Allen.

ALLEN   I shook the doctor's hand, wishing that I could deliver the secret handshake. The doctor looked away from me and focused on my father. I felt that Dr. Mubatto saw me as a failure, as a spoiled son, too selfish to join the Great Brotherhood.

[*The lights fade as* HELENA *plays the Gigue from Biber's Sonata No. 5 in A major. The light on her is stronger than before, she is more visibly "present."*]

FOUR

A Poem for my Father

1. Last Dreaming

[HILT *is in the dreamscape. His eyes are closed.*]

HILT   -I know, Mary, I know. But what can I do? She's my mother.

-I don't care if it rains the whole darn honeymoon.

-Smell nice. You taste salty.

-If our parents knew we were bare naked, they'd have a fit.

-Alright, my parents then.

-Mmm, salty. Like licking a cake of salt.

-Moo. Moo.

-A boy or a girl. Doesn't matter one way or the other.

-Little girl would be nice.

-I could play hockey with a boy though.

-Who's playing hockey over there?

-Mary?

-Here Laddie, here boy!

-You're all wet.

-Jesus.

-I don't know, Bert. I have to say I don't know.

-Did you leave it in the filing cabinet?

-Careful, Bert! There's water everywhere!

-It's not water. It's booze.

-Mary? Bert did something to the rain.

-Who's playing hockey over there? They'll drown.

-Allen, come back! You can't swim where they're skating. Those skates are sharp! Allen!

-Don't get lippy. Get down out of that tree! Now!

231

-Get your brother and get in here. It's suppertime.

-What? Oh, no.

-Yes, Dad. It's a pretty good looking eye. Better than the last one. They match up really well.

-I could tell better if you put it back in.

-Put it back before Allen and Bobby get here.

-Please.

-They're just boys. I don't want to scare them.

-Mary, don't let the boys in here.

-What can I do? He's my father.

-Quick, hide! I know him, he can hear you breathe.

-I don't know — behind the chesterfield.

-Where are the boys? Did I lose them?

-Holy-gods-a-war, we'll all be late for school!

-I'm right here, Dad. No, I'm not talking to anyone.

-Put your eye back.

-Allen, get out of here!

-Dad. Take your eye! Take it!

-Allen get out, get out! Get the hell out!

[HILT *opens his eyes*]

Where am I?

2. Salt Water

ALLEN   I almost said "no" to the reading because I've never gotten along with the other poet on the program. He reviewed my first book.

I read a poem about my grandfather. About his blindness, his inability to cry, and the irony of him swimming in salt water. I became aware of

Helena's eyes when I read the last stanza.

"His arms are pulling him through the unseen
     sea
pulling him furiously through calm salt water.
The sun on the bay heats the water warm as
     blood,
and blinds us."

HELENA   Your grandfather poem reminded me of home.
                Sunday afternoons when my father took us
                swimming.

ALLEN   Where was home?

HELENA   Nova Scotia. Roseway. You've never heard of it
                — it's very small.

ALLEN   She left when she was 19, first for Montreal,
                then Boston, then Toronto.

HELENA   I was lucky. A violinist who'd played with the
                Boston Symphony spent her summers near our
                house.

ALLEN   Her next recital will be broadcast on the radio.
                The gay man with her is her accompanist. He is
                also the brother of the poet I dislike.

HELENA   My father would leave us all on the beach and
                go swimming so far out that we couldn't see
                him anymore. Scared me to death.

ALLEN   Helena, her three sisters and their unhappy
                mother collecting shells, sand dollars, sea
                urchins ...

233

I find myself telling her that in many ways this is a poem about my own father.

HELENA   Then why didn't you put him in it?

ALLEN   I don't know, it's always been difficult with my father. I don't like myself very much when I try to write about him.

HELENA   Do you see him very often?

ALLEN   Well, no, I mean, he died. A while ago.

HELENA   Oh, I'm sorry. It's just that ... you seemed to be talking about him in the present tense.

ALLEN   Everyone else was crowded around the other poet, so we stood together talking about the East Coast, about our fathers, about music and poetry.

HELENA   Sylvia Plath still matters to me. I understand what you're saying and I don't disagree, but those poems matter. I read "Ariel" the year that I left home.

ALLEN   The poet has left with his brother, the room is almost empty.

HELENA   I'm glad now that Calvin dragged me here. Even though we had to sit through that bloodless crap his brother calls poetry.

ALLEN   I like this woman more and more.

HELENA   Can I give you a lift somewhere?

ALLEN   In the car we talk and talk, and I feel that my
         words are poor substitutes for my hands, my
         mouth. I want so much to kiss her, but I don't. I
         invite her to dinner, the next day.

         [HELENA *has left*.]

ALLEN   The things we have in common:

         A longing for salt water

         The sense that, long after they have left our
         lives, we continue to disappoint our fathers

         Andrew Marvell, Emily Dickinson, Elizabeth
         Bishop, Heinrich Biber, and Bach.

         The fact that within a month we are as
         comfortable with each other's bodies as we are
         with our own.

         In the spring, she tells me that she is pregnant
         and I can't believe how much I have been
         longing for my life to change.

3. Awake

         [HILT *is outside the dreamscape*.]

HILT   Mary?
         My chest
         Couch
         Hockey game
         Chest
         Why can't I move?
         Nothing is moving

the whole works
goddam chest —
Holy-gods-a-war
stupid heart!

Calm down
just calm down
it'll go away
away
calm yourself
away

No!
My whole life

End it all
heart attack
couch hockey game
dead
pearly gates

Mary
the boys
insurance
the will
mess in the garage
never got around to fixing the cellar door
scared shitless

4. Family

ALLEN   We went to visit Mom the week before she sold
            the old house. I left Helena in the back yard
            with Elizabeth. It was a hot day and our
            daughter was splashing in the wash tub, playing
            with some shells she'd found on the beach. She

talks to them, in the serious voice of a little mother talking to her dolls. She is so little, and so very beautiful. She looks like Helena and like pictures of my mother when she was a girl. Something about the shape of her mouth reminds me of Dad. Elizabeth and my mother adore each other, and for three days now Mom has been spoiling her rotten.

I want our daughter to hold all of this deep inside her. To remember this house, to keep this time with her grandmother shiny and forever.

Mom and I were alone in the kitchen. I was talking to her about how different everything is with Elizabeth in my life, about the thrills and terror of being a father. I said that some days I was worried about doing everything wrong.

My mother nodded. She was looking right at me when she said, "Remember the time we found those terrible books under Allen's mattress?"

I realized, in that moment, that I was no longer her son, that I was somehow my father, and I was too frightened to correct her. I just sat there not knowing what to do. "Mom," I finally said. "It's me, Allen."

She looked embarrassed, then she started speaking about the night before he died. They'd gone for their walk after supper, down to the wharf. Dad was talking about the summer I'd come home to be with him. The summer Mom went out and got stranded in Moose Jaw. "He told me you had a couple of really good talks," she said.

I couldn't bear to contradict her. Elizabeth saves
me by running in the back door. She's waving a
bleached, perfect sand dollar. "Treasure," she
says, "I found treasure."

5. Heaven

HILT

Mary
upstairs
upstairs sleeping
Oh, God Mary
safe as can be in bed with you
your legs between my legs between your legs
saving me from Mom and Dad
whatever you saw in me, I almost feel that you
put it there, because before you I didn't feel like
I was worth knowing
never alone with you
alone with Mom and Dad
never you

"not good enough"
Mom said
no one would have been
Good-byes at the back door
Mom's eyes
big sad dog eyes every single time I left that
yard
guilt, holy gods-a-war
she wrote the book

had to live with Dad
drive anyone crazy

wasn't always though
sandbar

238

sand castle
flowers
daisies on the turrets
devil's paint brush she put there
lining the little roads for my wagons
gave me her comb for a drawbridge
like being a kid again she said
she was so happy, she said
"the happiest little girl"

but Dad? little boy?
all I know is the scissors
never even said if he remembered seeing
never mentioned
old blind man till the day he died
died, dead
pearly gates

pearly gates —
last thing I need
Mom and Dad with wings on
would they even give wings to a blind man?
fly straight into something

be able to see, I suppose
first time since he was five
see me for the first time

sandcastle
shoe lace
scissors
not one smile in seventy years
scissors, then night
always night
pushing me away
always alone

never knew what I knew
Mary
on my knees in the pantry
my ear against her belly
the boys' heart beats inside her
and all my life is starting over

the boys grown up and gone
Bobby and his wife
a good girl if she'd only shut up
but Allen
Allen, Allen
always pushing
pushing me away

6. Giver and Receiver Meet

ALLEN   Helena and Elizabeth go back to Toronto and I
stay on at the old house. Bobby and his wife
arrive and we get started. Mom tries to help,
tries to be delighted when we show her things
that none of us have seen for years. A doll from
her childhood, Bobby's teddy bear, Dad's
masonic apron. We work for days. Packing the
things she will take to her seniors' apartment,
sorting out which things are for yard sale, which
for auction.

Tucked away in an old strongbox are the things
my father could never throw away. Some old
photos, a ration book from the war, an old
masonic badge. There is a stack of all the
birthday and Father's Day cards that we ever
gave him. One of them I remember from
primary school: faded brown construction
paper, rounded corners — it's supposed to look

like a wallet and has red yarn threaded through the holes I carefully punched around the edges.

Inside my greeting card wallet is the first poem I ever wrote:

"Roses are red
Poppies are too
You are my father
Happy Father's Day to you"

The construction paper takes me back to Miss Rodd's classroom, to the way I would order my desktop: pencils in the wooden groove, scissors and eraser beside them, glue in the old inkwell hole in the upper right hand corner. I remember sitting at my desk feeling the way that I imagined Dad felt sitting at his desk at the office: filled with accomplishment and importance, a king of business.

I remember my father coming home after work — remember waiting on the front steps for Bert Seaman's big car to pull up.

I remember going for walks with my father, remember Dad holding my hand while we drop sticks into a ditch swollen with fast moving water. "Careful, careful," he said — he always seemed to be telling me to be careful. When he told me that there was so much water because of heavy snows melting in the woods above the town, it was more than information: the connection between deep snow in the woods and the water rushing past our feet was poetry. The idea of it made me shiver with pleasure.

Also in his strongbox is a bible that belonged to my grandmother. It is filled with things she could not bear to throw away.

A post card from her sister in Boston. Inspirational poems she clipped from the newspaper.

An envelope containing four locks of my father's baby hair tied with blue ribbons and two tiny baby teeth.

I hold in my middle age hand all that remains of my father's body — little treasures that he has allowed my grandmother to hand to me over so many years. His curls are so fine, and golden, and the teeth gleam in the evening light, tiny milk pearls.

7. Gray's Elegy

HILT

Allen
every damn thing you do
push me
writing
poetry
no future there
don't end up scraping
bowing
scraping
a real job
comfort
no kowtowing
the likes of Bert Seaman
make some money
some comfort

not poetry
poetry
poetry
whatsat poem?
memorized it
Miss Leaman
Aberdeen School
>   "The curfew tolls the knell of parting
>   day;"

memorized the whole damn thing
verse after verse
must've been — what — twenty of them
no, more
grade what? eight?
verse after verse
quite the thing
still can

>   "The curfew tolls the knell of parting
>   day;
>   The lowing herd winds slowly o'er the
>   lea;
>   The ploughman homeward plods his
>   weary way;
>   And leaves the world to darkness and to
>   me."

Ha

>   "leaves the world to darkness and to me"

Poor Miss Leaman
I can see her yet
she knew about Dad
his temper
I know she knew
the way she was nice to me
Miss Leaman
I loved that poem
that's a poem

243

rhymes
and that — whatsit?
iambic that's it
iambic something
Allen, your stuff — I don't have a clue
      "and leaves the world to darkness and
      to me"
that line, big one, whatsit?
      The paths of glory lead but to the grave
that's it
      "and leaves the world to darkness and
      to me"
Ha

      "The *something something something*
      pomp of power
      And all that beauty, all that *something*
      gave
      Await, alike the inevitable hour
      The paths of glory lead but to the grave"

Something like that
I love that poem
words
my boy
more than words
like hands
more than hands when they're Mary's
boys more than boys when they're your own

8. Cemetery

ALLEN   Not even my mother comes here very often.
      It's too sad for her I suppose. And Bobby
      hasn't been here since the funeral. Says he
      doesn't need to. But I take a break from
      packing up the house, drive down. There it is:

his name, the dates, the Masonic emblem.

It's hard to believe he's been gone for ten years. When Mom went to bed he was watching the hockey game; when she got up in the morning the TV was still on and she said that he looked like he was asleep on the couch.

My grandfather is here, too, next to his wife: blind Fred, homely Bessie, both laid in her family plot. My sister, who lived for half a breath, is buried with them. Just across the way, on the other side of the lilac bush, is the big pink stone that Olive Seaman erected for Bert. She's there now, too, and near them, what was left of Billy after he was burned to cinders in the fire set by a motorcycle gang who didn't like the way he was selling their drugs. He was in his early twenties.

All of these stories are a part of my daughter's legacy. And many of them are things that I want to protect her from. Not because they're family secrets, not that, but because they might erode her picture of the world as a wonderful place. Filled with treasure.

The spring before Dad died I phoned home to tell him I was having a book of poetry published. "Wellsir," he said, and that was that.

When I was in college, I believed that I was smarter than him, more tolerant than him, better than him. I never had a really good talk with him.

Sometimes I write for days and days and nothing comes of it. Nothing.

But sometimes when I'm writing, I can sense, I don't know, a vagueness that I know will take shape. A brief glimpse of an idea, maybe even a piece of a line. I can almost touch it. And a certainty begins to settle around it and — I know this probably won't make any sense to you at all — but I can *feel* what it's about.

And the wonderful thing — a little miracle, really — I have to wait a bit before I start working on it. There's a period of anticipation — like waiting for Helena to come to bed. I know that the poem, like Helena and Elizabeth, like ... well, like you and Mom and Bobby, the poem is already a part of me. I don't mean that writing it will be easy, but it's waiting for me to find it, to discover its peculiar rules and geography, to search out the words and realize something by writing it.

[ALLEN *lies down as* HELENA *begins to play the Saraband from Biber's Sonata No. 5 in A major.*]

The Dream

[HELENA *continues to play.* ALLEN *is sleeping when* HILT *comes and stands at his feet.*]

ALLEN   Dad? Dad?

[HILT *leans against* ALLEN*'s feet and* ALLEN *lifts his father into the air. They let go of each others' hands.*]

HILT   *(Gently)* Careful. Be careful.

[HILT *stretches out his arms. Fade.*]

246